The Making of the Mayor

The Making of the Mayor

CHICAGO 1983

editors

MELVIN G. HOLLI *and* PAUL M. GREEN

GRAND RAPIDS, MICHIGAN

WILLIAM B. EERDMANS PUBLISHING COMPANY

_R00720 55893_

In Memory of Milton Rakove   1918–1983

Library of Congress Cataloging in Publication Data

Main entry under title:

The Making of the mayor, Chicago, 1983.
    1. Chicago (Ill.)—Mayors—Election—Addresses,
essays, lectures.   2. Elections—Illinois—Chicago—
Addresses, essays, lectures.   3. Washington, Harold,
1922-   —Addresses, essays, lectures.   4. Chicago—
Politics and government—1951-   —Addresses, essays,
lectures.   I. Holli, Melvin G.   II. Green, Paul Michael.
JS718.3.M34   1984   324.9773'11033   84-5998
ISBN 0-8028-7047-3

Contents

List of Figures, Tables, and Charts

Preface

"The Making of the Mayor: Chicago 1983" began simultaneously as an idea for a book and a concept for a conference. When planning began early in 1982, the pre-election period showed all of the signs of developing into one of those historic, watershed elections that may serve in the future to demarcate one period of Chicago's governmental history from another. The electric political atmosphere crackled with speculation: Would Rich restore the Daley dynasty? Would an Eastern European ethnic get into the line of mayoral succession? What about that fat and formidable multimillion-dollar war chest owned by the incumbent?

Subsequently—in the postelection period—the conference was held on May 20, 1983 at the Chicago Historical Society and was sponsored by the Society, the University of Illinois at Chicago and at Urbana, Governors State University, and *Illinois Issues* magazine. It proved to be an illuminating and intellectually engaging event. Several of the essays in this book were first presented in draft form at the conference, where they benefited immensely from rigorous scholarly and public criticism as well as acclaim. Among the panelists so vitally important to that process were Charles Branham, Bernard Brommel, Samuel K. Gove, Richard Jensen, Eugene Kennedy, Paul Kleppner, Michael Lennon, Edward Marciniak, Louis M. Masotti, Edward Mazur, William McCready, Gerald McWhorter, and Barri Watkins, along with Sharon Alter, Phil Krone, John Madigan, Thomas Roeser, Norman Ross, and Luis Salces.

Other chapters in the book—Robert McClory's "Up from Obscurity: Harold Washington," Richard Day's "Polling in the 1983 Mayoral Election," and Don Rose's "How the Election Was Won"— were commissioned outside the conference but were subjected to the same rigorous standards of criticism before being integrated into the text.

We wish to thank the sponsoring organizations and participants listed above, as well as Ellsworth H. Brown, director of the Chicago Historical Society, who provided us with an ideal public forum in which to try out these ideas before committing them to print.

Introduction

The opening chapter, entitled "Up from Obscurity," is intended as a general introduction to a candidate who was poorly known to Chicagoans even on election eve. The story of how an enigmatic and obscure state and national legislator soared out of nowhere to become the most nationally visible black politician in the slipstream of media consciousness during the winter and spring of 1983 is a fascinating one. So elemental was the information on mayoral candidate Harold Washington that campaign puffery and paeans of praise were often passed off as hard facts in the press. Washington himself was aware of his lack of citywide recognition right up to the televised debates, saying: "Until then I was practically an unknown quantity. They [the debates] represented the only way for me to project myself. . . ." Even after the primary, solid information on Washington was not easy to come by. Unlike the incumbent, Mayor Jane Byrne, who had been the subject of two book-length studies and numerous articles, interviews, and analyses, candidate Washington remained a kind of billboard figure who, according to his campaign aides, was a cross between George and Booker T. Washington but, according to his detractors, was a "race baiter" and a "crook."[1] Part of the painful process of the public's getting to know Harold came by way of dramatic revelations that his opponents dug up—revelations of a suspended law license, tax delinquencies, and nonpayment of bills. Even after the campaign, public knowledge of Chicago's first black mayor remained remarkably sketchy and incomplete.[2] The new mayor, who prized and guarded his personal life, seemed content to leave it that way.

Thus Robert McClory's essay, although clearly not the last word on the subject, is a good introduction to an articulate black man who beat City Hall; it intends not only to put the record straight but to put the record forth. As McClory points out, disturbing questions about the Washington record still remain to be answered, such as why Washington failed to file his tax returns for four years. Among Washington's stock answers have been "stupidity" or "just plain forgot," which have struck some less than charitable critics as not quite credible, since tax day and Washington's birthday both fall on April 15. Yet on other issues, as McClory points out, Washington is fully understandable to any city watcher as the quintessential political man. Why did he run even against formidable odds? "Politics is like shooting pool or eating Cracker Jacks. Once you start, you just can't stop," says the mayor.

Professor Paul M. Green's examination of the mayoral primary and its restrospective connection to the ongoing stream of Chicago's mayoral history adds a vital and important historical dimension. Primaries, as Green points out, have historically served the "outs" and the near "outs" against the "ins"; in time-honored fashion, the February 22nd—George Washington's birthday—primary served to bring the "outs" in. Green's chapter sensitively delineates the time-worn Democratic party ritual of slatemaking; shows Byrne on the attack with her saturation TV campaign; and follows the campaign through the debates and to the newspaper endorsements. Green takes note of the continuous, nonstop negative bombardment of Byrne by the two major dailies, which, even in the process of endorsing young Daley, continued to hurl barbs at the incumbent mayor—a campaign that tore gaping holes into critical support areas for Byrne.

When the chips were down and votes were ebbing away to Byrne's black opponent, the Democratic machine forces made their calculated but desperate last gamble with its pitch that "a vote for Daley is a vote for Washington . . . it is a racial thing," which had an unanticipated and paradoxical effect: it hurt Daley but slightly, helped Washington enormously, and probably lost for Byrne her black vote and the election. Losing an election is clearly no fun, for as Jane Byrne reminisced later: "I went to the polling place sixteen points ahead and woke up three points behind. . . . It was like we were all in the intensive care unit of a hospital watching the machine. It was like when the doctor calls you aside. I felt like a member of the family had died."[3] Race was the key to this campaign, argues Professor Green, but with a perverse twist, for "if Harold Washington had been a white, he would not have *entered* let alone *won* the 1983 Chicago Democratic mayoral primary."

In a postmortem of the elections, Green ponders how effectively Washington will be able to govern the city and suggests that one of his greatest obstacles may not be the City Council's opposition but rather the heated crusade-like passions unleashed by the "movement" people who helped put Harold in and who view political compromise as betrayal. Green concludes on a reflective note, suggesting that political psychologists and psycho-biographers may have a field day for years to come puzzling over the Jane Byrne phenomenon. For it appears that Mayor Byrne goaded young Rich Daley into becoming her challenger with the thought that she would destroy him politically in the primary, thereby eliminating forever the threat of a Daley restoration and leaving her the rightful heir to the Daley legend.

Chicago is a marvelous city in which to study politics. It is sometimes said that Chicago is the one city in America where politics competes with night baseball and sex as a topic of keen interest and passionate discussion. That is more than just a rhetorical flourish: for whereas the voter turnout for national elections runs about 53 percent, Chicago voters have transformed their passion into votes and in comparable elections have turned out at the 70 percent plus level during the last decade. Chicago's black voters topped even that in 1983, when they pushed the turnout level to an astonishing peak of 80 percent.

Low voter turnout among minorities has been attributed in the past to a number of factors, including socioeconomic status (SES), political cynicism, conspiracy, voter apathy, and the like. Professor Michael Preston examines the black voting surge of the 1980s that culminated in the Washington election. In a retrospective look at voter behavior, Preston argues that while blacks supported the Democratic machine during the period between 1955 and 1979, their low turnout was an indicator of growing dissatisfaction with the Democratic organization. Black voting consistently lagged behind citywide or white voting through 1977, but it picked up noticeably in 1979. The lower voter turnout in black middle-class wards than in black lower-income wards seems on the face of it to contradict the comfortable paradigm that SES explains most voter turnout behavior.

The especially sharp decline in middle-class black voters in the 1977 mayoralty leads Preston to argue that the most knowledgeable black voters were responding rationally to what they perceived as the invincibility of the political machine. Preston's findings, which were derived from demographic data, run counter to the conventional wisdom that lack of political knowledge is the best predictor of nonvoting.[4] Professor Preston makes his case especially persuasive by displaying graphs that cover the period: they show that the presumably same Chicago black voters who diminished their voter turn-outs in mayoral elections maintained relatively high turnouts in presidential elections during the same period of time. Preston refers to this gap between presidential and mayoral elections as the "un-used" voting potential. Other factors in lower-income black wards that depressed turnout were weak ward organization, a transient population, and lack of leadership, in addition to the common SES explanations.

Jane Byrne's primary triumph over regular Democrat Michael Bilandic proved instrumental in galvanizing the black vote and dem-onstrating how that "unused" black vote potential could affect the outcome. The black middle class had returned to voter participation. As Professor Preston points up, the election of Harold Washington as mayor in 1983 may be viewed as the culmination of a black dis-satisfaction with the Chicago Democratic machine that had been building for years. Washington and his crusade's victory over the most powerful city political machine in the nation has given the Chicago election visibility far beyond what a single big-city election normally commands.

Richard Day's insightful chapter on public opinion polling in the 1983 elections captures the incredible volatility of the Chicago electorate—how the political fortunes of various candidates could rise and fall in remarkably short periods of time. One of the most dramatic and controversial aspects of the campaign was Byrne strat-egists' realization too late that their real opponent was Washington. When they tried to capitalize on that fact, they were labeled "racists" and probably lost the primary on this misfired stratagem. The Wash-ington camp, although often in confusion, deftly exploited this tac-tical blunder of his opponents and headed them off at the pass in the grey dawn of election morning. As Day points out, the Harold Washington forces broke through the Byrne lines on the opinion charts at the very last moment, closed the gap, and snatched victory on election day. Although Chicagoans in general might have guessed at this drama in the making, the public opinion polls would record these voter shifts with the precision of generals mapping a campaign.

As Mr. Day shows, the general election between Democrat Washington and Republican Bernard Epton provided fewer sur-prises to the pollsters, but it was still important to track because the mass partisan defection that occurred during the primary might be repeated in the general election. That proved to be the case when Washington won what Chicagoans call a "squeaker" on April 12. The exit polls provided an excellent indicator of the victory that was building and also provided the public with a sophisticated breakdown of voter demographics that the raw election data could not. The polls, Day asserts, were valuable tools for measuring the salience and nonsalience of issues such as the candidate's record, gender, race, and partisan loyalty in one of Chicago's truly historic and memorable elections. Day concludes with the observation that as the Chicago electorate becomes more fragmented and often single-issue-minded, and as candidates begin to appeal to discrete and often contradictory interest groups within the Democratic party structure, public opinion polling will become an increasingly important tool for understanding what may be a new and highly pluralized Windy City polity.

A nationally recognized expert on the influence of the media in politics, Professor Doris Graber has conducted a careful and scholarly content analysis of the Chicago print media during the primary and general elections. Graber and her coinvestigator, Sharon O'Donnell, set out to appraise the merits and deficiencies of news coverage by examining the metropolitan press (and selected television coverage) from several different vantage points, such as "policy" versus "hoopla and horse race"; the distribution of coverage among candidates; and the negative and positive story orientation of the various candidates. They found a qualitative and cumulative lack of balance in several dimensions. Professor Graber writes that the media's reporting strategies exaggerated inflammatory comments and in fact "projected a racially focused campaign from the moment Washington entered the contest." As early as November 29, the Chicago *Tribune* ran a feature editorial by Leanita McClain entitled "The Racial Truth of Politics," which asked Chicagoans to "acknowledge that race is going to be an issue whether anyone wants it to be or not." She urged Chicagoans: "Don't try to sweep it aside, deal with it."[5] Other potential issues such as gender, "dynasty," religion, and even finance were mostly ignored in the election coverage.

Why do such major imbalances in coverage come about? Professor Graber responds: "The answer is that newspeople produce them. They pick and choose whom they wish to cover and whom they wish to ignore. They also select the individuals whose views they will report." The news "filtered" through such perspectives communicated to readers that the battle was between "Bad Jane, Good Richie, and Simon-Pure Harold" during the primary. During the general election Harold, "now a little less pure, was joined by 'Decent Bernie,' who had been largely a nonperson" during the primary. Graber also introduces the concept of "medialities," or pseudo-events that are blown out of their true proportion by media attention.

Graber and O'Donnell conclude with a provocative series of findings. Among them is the conclusion that even though the press unleashed a one-sided, unremitting, and nonstop assault on Jane Byrne and let her two opponents off almost scot-free, and even though they overplayed the race issue, the news coverage of the 1983 mayoralty was slightly above average. Anticipating loud protestations by newspeople, in which they argue that they simply "mirror" the events of the time, Graber would answer that newspeople are not "passive" receptors but control the substance of stories, decide which subjects merit attention and which do not, and control the manner in which these subjects are presented. Journalists who are often "professional and merciless critics of others, are surprisingly sensitive when it comes to criticism directed against them," Graber adds. Readers will find this scientific and surgical dissection of the news blizzard and the political fire storm that they passed through both instructive and revealing.

Veteran city watcher, writer, and political consultant Don Rose takes us on a tour of the campaign strategies used by both candidates in the general election. Rose offers an ingenious interpretation to explain how Bernard Epton got into the mayoral race, which begins with the legislative cutback amendment. Had single-member districts not been enacted, Rose argues, Epton would never have gotten into a citywide race but would have been content to remain an enlightened progressive Republican from a sinecure made possible by the old cumulative voting scheme once used in Illinois. Epton's background also goes a long way in explaining how the campaign strains began to show visibly on the candidate in a knockdown, no-holds-barred, rough-and-tough Chicago election. With insight and some humor, Rose also covers campaign snafus, stuttering start-ups, and false starts and stops, such as the Byrne write-in and some of the hit-or-miss and seat-of-the-pants stratagems that punctuated the campaign. Some of the Washington campaign's gambles—such as meeting the bogus morals charge head-on, raising questions about Bernard Epton's mental health, and bringing a parade of national Democrats in to endorse him (including the tarnished Bert Lance)— were high-risk strategies that could have backfired and hurt Washington badly; as it turned out, they helped him. The issue of Epton's stolen medical records, for example, could have been exploited as a mini-Watergate, Ellsberg-style break-in—which could have hurt Washington fatally in the very liberal lakefront areas where he hoped to win the election. Although viewing the campaign from a Washington perspective, Rose is judicious and balanced in his presentation and sufficiently objective to concede that a black other than Washington "might have had an easier time winning, but it is also safe to say that a white candidate other than Epton, running a less strident campaign, might have wound up mayor."

An expert on Chicago's Democratic machine, the late Professor Milton Rakove (deceased, November 1983) undertook to examine the current status of that institution and to speculate on its future. When Rakove wrote his insightful book on the machine, *Don't Make No Waves, Don't Back No Losers,* Mayor Richard J. Daley was at the peak of his powers, and Chicago was the city that worked: the garbage was picked up, toilets flushed, and even the Chicago Transit Authority sometimes ran on time—all under the apparent anachronistic dinosaur called the "Chicago machine." Muckraker reformist Lincoln Steffens, who made a trip to the Soviet Union in 1919 and exclaimed, "I have seen the future and it works," could have added, had he lived long enough to visit Chicago a half century later, "I have seen the past and that works too." But since the passing of Daley it has worked less and less well. Professor Rakove describes the machine as having gone downhill for some time. Even the chairman of the Cook County Democratic Central Committee concedes that the "organization has been running at about 40 percent effectiveness for a long time. I feel we ran about 60 percent this time," he said of the 1982 fall election. Yet the death of the machine has been prematurely announced by civic uplifters, good government reformers, and lakefront liberals since it came into being a half century ago. Popular Chicago radio host and author Studs Terkel told *The New York Times*, "The celebrated Chicago machine is no longer celebrated. It is a junk heap." *Vox populi* had triumphed. The new mayor, Harold Washington, clearly thinks that it is on the critical list; he announced boldly at his inaugural that the "machine is mortally wounded and like a mortally wounded animal will drift off into the woods to die."[6] In addition, a series of court orders called the "Shakman decrees," which forbid patronage hiring and firing, have shackled the machine so that it cannot secure pelf and place for its foot soldiers. But Rakove warns that objective observers must wait and see, for the jury is still out. Furthermore, he cautions that the machine is capable of adaptation and metamorphosis.

William Grimshaw's seminal essay not only agrees with Matthias "Paddy" Bauler's aphorism—"Chicago ain't ready for reform yet"—but goes one better by arguing that Chicago may be less ready for reform now than when Paddy uttered his truism. Reform is not only based on class but is also a cultural phenomenon, and the middle-class Protestants and Jews who spearheaded classical municipal reform have made an exodus for the suburbs. Left behind, according to Grimshaw, are only a few oddball pockets of reform in Hyde Park and on the lakeshore, anachronisms in an increasingly poor and black city. There are simply not enough middle-class Protestants and Jews to sustain a municipal reform movement of the traditional stripe. Grimshaw traces the shape and types of reform in Chicago politics, which he labels "class reform," "party reform," and a new type which he calls "status reform." Class reform typically emphasized clean government, businesslike efficiency, and the merit system; party reform was a more recent type exemplified by the efforts of William Singer and others to open up the Democratic party to newcomers and outsiders. The third in Grimshaw's typology, "status reform," derives from a black "lower-class reform style," which, Grimshaw asserts, is primarily concerned with the redistribution of the benefits of government to blacks and other have-nots, those who parallel, ironically, the beneficiaries of the old machine—the white ethnics. This reform style, Grimshaw says, originates from a black "ethic of fairness" nourished in black churches. If a new Harold Washington policy aims at a "downward distribution" of loaves and fishes, then Grimshaw warns the new mayor that he should be careful to "redistribute equity on class and not racial grounds." Grimshaw concludes with the observation that "race has replaced reform" as the "great political divide" in Chicago. Whether the "ethic of fairness" is simply a fancy name for a black version of old-fashioned patronage or whether it is a doctrine that can stand on its own two feet as a separate type in the reform morphology[7] is something the reader and history will have to decide as the Washington administration leaves its mark on the city.

---

1. Chicago *Tribune,* February 24, 1983; Mike Royko, Chicago *Sun-Times,* April 12, 1983.

2. *Dollars and Cents,* IX (April-May 1983). Florence H. Levinsohn has written a paean of praise to Washington and a passionate condemnation of all who opposed him as "racists." *Harold Washington: A Political Biography* (Chicago, 1983).

3. Carol Oppenheim interview of Jane Byrne, Chicago *Tribune,* May 6, 1983.

4. Roger Fox, "Why Chicago's Blacks Do Not Register and Vote" (Chicago Urban League, September 1981), 11, 16.

5. McClain would later write an article for the Washington *Post* entitled "How Chicago Taught Me to Hate Whites," *Illinois Issues*, IX (October 1983), 37.

6. Chicago *Tribune,* November 6, 1982; *The New York Times,* April 17, 1983; Washington quoted in Chicago *Tribune,* April 13, 1983.

7. See Melvin G. Holli, "Varieties of Urban Reform," in *American Urban History,* Alexander B. Callow, Jr., ed. (New York, 1982).

The Election . . .

I

Up from Obscurity: Harold Washington

ROBERT McCLORY

"Politics is like shooting pool or eating Cracker Jacks. Once you start, you just can't stop."

—Harold Washington

During Harold Washington's thirty-year apprenticeship in the world of politics, Dempsey Travis, his friend and former classmate at Roosevelt College, would occasionally urge him to shift into the more rewarding realm of real estate. Travis, who was amassing a fortune as a Southside Chicago mortgage banker, failed to understand Washington's dogged dedication to a profession that provided so few visible earthly rewards. But Washington always said no, recalled Travis: he didn't want money; he wanted politics.

Indeed, dedication to politics has always been a characteristic of Chicago's new mayor. And so has disregard for money. These two characteristics help explain how he quietly and steadily moved up through the ranks until, in 1983, he found himself in the right place at the right time—and how he very nearly fumbled the opportunity.

Harold Washington is a remarkable man of paradoxes and enigmas. At times he seems as wise as a serpent and at others as simple as a dove—yet always stimulating and incredibly eloquent. "No matter how he performs as mayor," noted one political observer on the day after the election, "the city's vocabulary is bound to expand."

He was born on April 15, 1922, the fifth of the ten children of Roy and Bertha Washington. His father was a lawyer, a Methodist minister, a police court prosecutor, and an active 1st Ward Democratic precinct captain under Mike Sneed, the first black ward committeeman in Chicago. So prominent was Roy Washington on the black South Side of the 1920s and 1930s that old-timers remember him as "Mr. 48th St." His loyalty to the Chicago political organization was richly rewarded when he was appointed assistant city corporation counsel, one of the first of his race to hold that office.

Harold Washington has always been reluctant to discuss details of his family life with the press, but old friends say his father and mother were divorced when the boy was still very young. Harold, along with three other siblings, went with his father, who later remarried, thus extending and somewhat complicating family life. For a short period, Harold attended St. Benedict the Moor Grammar School in Milwaukee, apparently as a boarding student, then transferred to the old Forrestville Elementary School near his home in Chicago's 3rd Ward. He moved on to DuSable High School, where he distinguished himself as a high hurdler and a middleweight boxer, and he earned money in his spare time setting up pins at a Northside bowling alley.

To this day Washington considers his father the one and only real hero in life. "I was raised on the streets of the South Side and wended my way through this horrible public school system," he told an audience during the mayoral campaign. "I was very fortunate. My father was my role model. He was a real man, he was a good man. For many years he was not only my father, he was my mother. And so I knew who Santa Claus was. He came home every night, put his feet under the table and had dinner with me."[2]

Washington's formal education was interrupted by World War II. He served four years as an Air Force engineer, two of them in the Pacific, and attained the rank of first sergeant by the time of his honorable discharge. Under the G.I. Bill, he enrolled at newly opened Roosevelt College in downtown Chicago, where he majored in political science. It was there that he was first noticed—for refusing to join any of the regular fraternities on the grounds that they discriminated against blacks. He formed an independent fraternity, whose fate no one seems to recall. Yet, despite the ruckus, Washington was elected president of the overwhelmingly white senior class and was also president of the student council.

Besides Dempsey Travis, Washington's classmates at Roosevelt included Bennett Johnson, a publisher and veteran Chicago political independent, and Gus Savage, who so relished editing the Roosevelt student newspaper that he later founded his own Southside Chicago community newspaper, The Citizen. According to their associates, Washington and Savage, while chatting one day during their senior year about the sad state of local politics, both decided to become U.S. congressmen. Those decisions, incredibly enough, were both realized on the same day thirty-two years later, when Washington was elected to the U.S. House of Representatives from the First Illinois Congressional District and Savage from the Second.

During his college years Washington married his neighborhood sweetheart, but the couple was quietly divorced ten years later, in 1955. They had no children. Contacted by reporters during the mayoral campaign, Washington's former wife, now Mrs. Nancy Nesbitt of Memphis, said she held no bitterness toward him. "We were very good friends before our marriage," she said, "and we remain friends. If I were still in Chicago, I would vote for Harold. He's the best candidate—very intelligent, very conscientious."[3]

While he was still in his mid-twenties, friends regarded Harold Washington as something of an intellectual. "He was always a voracious reader," said one long-time associate. "He'd take a book on any subject off the library shelf—history, anthropology, medicine, anything—just devour it. And if there wasn't a book around, he'd read the ingredients on a bottle of aspirin or a tube of toothpaste. And the most amazing thing: he would remember everything he read!"[4]

With all that information filed away, young Washington became a popular conversationalist and a capable debater, with an amazing vocabulary that could wither his foes in mid-argument. With those credentials, appropriately enough, he announced his intention to become an attorney, and he pursued studies at Northwestern University School of Law, from which he graduated in 1952.

When Roy Washington died the next year, Harold took over his private law practice and succeeded him as assistant corporation counsel for the city—his formal introduction to the world of politics and government. He found it a fascinating world and soon became deeply involved in 3rd Ward affairs.

In the early 1960s he served as ~~an arbitrator~~ a judge for the Illinois Industrial Commission, but it was clear his career was to be in the political realm. He carefully studied the intricacies and mysteries of the Chicago machine under the 3rd Ward's alderman and Democratic committeeman of the time, the sad-eyed, sepulchral-voiced, war-horse Ralph Metcalfe. The two, however, never were close friends. Perhaps it was the mutual respect of two strong-willed men, but a certain wariness marked the relationship even while Washington was managing three of Metcalfe's aldermanic campaigns in the 1960s and later, two successful congressional races. Washington learned firsthand the fundamentals of using the powers of patronage, city services, friendship, threat, or whatever else it took to get elected. He also learned the lessons of organizational loyalty, of supporting the party line at all costs, of keeping your mouth shut in public. And in the midst of it he was infected by the incurable virus of politics. "Politics is like shooting pool or eating Cracker Jacks," he has said. "Once you start, you just can't stop."[5]

It was a priceless education, and it all seemed to be coming to fruition in 1964, when Metcalfe sponsored his prize pupil for a seat in the state legislature. Washington ran in the 26th District, which included Englewood, West Englewood, Grand Boulevard, and Woodlawn. With no family ties or outside interests, Washington seemingly had the ambition and freedom to go as far as he wanted within the existing limitations imposed by racism.

But no sooner was Washington installed in the Illinois General Assembly than word came back from Democratic loyalists in Springfield that the freshman was not what they had expected. He wasn't a "crazy independent," of course, but his questioning attitude and his refusal on some occasions to obey orders contrasted noticeably with the traditional zombie-like behavior of his black colegislators. And as the term went on, Washington was seen operating on his own more and more often, attempting to change people's minds, working out little ad hoc blocs for specific bills. But since most of his efforts had to do with curtailing business exploitation in the black community and with furthering equal opportunity, organization complaints against the man were generally muttered behind closed doors.

No one has ever fully explained this sudden switch in allegiance, although Washington has given hints. He was uncomfortable all of those years under Metcalfe, he once acknowledged, collecting IOUs from poor people and expecting a payback. He has mentioned one occasion when he helped solve a personal problem for a 3rd Ward resident who was a Jehovah's Witness. When the man asked Washington what he could do in return, Washington told him to register for the upcoming election—even though he was well aware Jehovah's Witnesses are expected to shun all political activity. The man complied, and Washington said he was long distressed at having forced someone to violate his conscience.[6] Once down in the General Assembly and 180 miles away from Metcalfe's dominance, it appears, his reluctance to shove people around for political gain came to the surface.

In 1969, after Washington's first two terms in the state house, the consensus in the Cook County Democratic organization was that he had wasted his chance for a long career. He lacked that indispensable "team spirit," that ability to meld invisibly with his fellows that marked a good machine Democrat. For the first time the term "maverick" and that dreaded epithet "independent" were being hung on Washington by news reporters. Party chairman Richard J. Daley decided he had to go. But slatemakers were unable to remove Washington from the ballot. Despite his cussed orneriness, Washington was highly regarded and extremely visible in his poverty-stricken Southside district. He might have ignored some fundamental political lessons, but he had remembered the part about staying in touch with constituents. He won another term with ease.

From that point forward the relationship between Washington and his political superiors, especially Metcalfe, could only be described as ambiguous. He picked his own causes, and he voted the way he wanted. If his choices reflected the party line, fine; if they did not, he did not seem to give a damn. Meanwhile, his reputation as a tough, innovative legislator was growing even as his stock with the organization was deteriorating. Not only was he the principal author of bills to put real teeth into the state's Fair Employment Practices Commission, to upgrade the Illinois Code of Corrections, to protect witnesses to crimes, to aid small businesses, and to help poor and elderly consumers—but he personally steered them through the appropriate committees and saw them passed into law.

In 1976, when he ran for the state senate (also from the 26th District) and won, his popularity in the black community grew. His name and face appeared regularly in the Chicago *Defender* and other black-oriented publications, and Southsiders referred to him casually as "my senator." January 15 became a holiday in Illinois in honor of Dr. Martin Luther King because of a bill introduced by Harold Washington. Some 10 percent of state contracts was set aside for black contractors—thus bringing $600 million into the black community—because of a bill introduced by Washington. Citizens were often the victims of unequal currency exchange rates until the legislature passed a reform that was designed and sponsored by Washington. In the midst of a devastating financial crunch, Provident Hospital, an historic black institution in Chicago, was saved through a $15 million state grant engineered by Washington.

One time Washington spearheaded a boycott that delayed the opening of the state legislature for six weeks. The issue was whether blacks would choose their own legislative spokesperson or whether the Democratic powers, particularly Senator Richard M. Daley, would make the choice. Eventually, Daley and company backed off, and the black caucus named its own man.

A string of awards and honorary degrees started coming Washington's way in the 1970s, including the citation as one of the ten outstanding state legislators in *Chicago* magazine (based on a poll of reporters, lobbyists, and fellow legislators) and an honorable mention in a similar poll by the Chicago *Sun-Times,* which called him "the most capable black in the legislature."[7] The thing about him was his uncluttered agenda, admitted veteran Springfield observers. A wheeler-dealer he was, but not for the normal goals of financial gain, power acquisition, or ego satisfaction. From the traditional machine point of view, his political perspective was incomprehensible.

In 1975, Washington and Metcalfe had an especially bitter falling out that never really healed. Black leaders of an independent stripe saw an opportunity to shake up Mayor Daley's apple cart by persuading Metcalfe to run in that year's Democratic mayoral primary. For a time Metcalfe appeared ready to go along. Then at the last moment he backed down, recommending that dissatisfied blacks cast their lot with William Singer, a white independent alderman. Metcalfe's behavior angered blacks, including Washington, who had labored to draft him. Washington was, in fact, so upset that he considered quitting politics altogether; but he decided to stay around and see what developed.

In 1976 Daley died, and those who had backed Metcalfe persuaded Washington to make a run for the mayor's office in the special election the next year. It was a shabby, hastily put together campaign with a shoestring budget. Washington got 11 percent of the vote and actually carried five black wards, although Michael Bilandic was the easy winner. Despite the loss (the only political defeat he has ever absorbed), Washington considered his fair showing a victory of sorts. He spoke of it as "a harbinger of things to come" in future elections, though he was not specific on that point.

Washington was well aware at that time that his apostasy from the machine was total and would probably never be forgiven. "I just gradually realized that I was kidding myself to believe I was going to do anything of meaningful value in the structure," he told a newsman. "I was getting little bills passed, but there was something bigger than that—this monster just had to be dealt with."[8]

The machine was beginning to fear Washington, and it made elaborate efforts to dump him before his popularity got out of hand. When he ran for re-election in 1978, James Taylor, his fellow legislator from the 26th District and a man sometimes criticized as the supreme local example of black subservience, persuaded two women named Washington (Sabrina and Denise) to run in the Democratic primary—in hopes of confusing voters into pulling the lever for the wrong Washington. One of the phantom Washingtons was ruled off the ballot because of defective petitions, but the other stayed on. With Taylor's precinct workers laboring overtime on behalf of the party's real choice, Clarence Berry, it was widely predicted that Washington's fourteen-year stay in the legislature was over. But somehow Harold Washington pulled it out—winning by a mere 239 votes over Berry.

The First District U.S. Congressional seat, which had been temporarily filled by Bennett Stewart following Metcalfe's sudden death in 1978, came up for election in 1980. And Washington, in the midst of his second term in the state senate, moved to widen his political base. He was opposed by a trio of powerful opponents, including incumbent Stewart, who had the backing of Mayor Byrne and the Democratic organization; John Stroger, a party loyalist with influential business friends, who was miffed when the party failed to slate him; and Ralph Metcalfe, Jr., running on his late father's coattails.

For Washington, the campaign served as a warmup for the mayoral battle that was to come three years later. Instead of concentrating on the declared contenders, he attacked Jane Byrne with relentless zeal. "They tell us no black person has the qualifications to be mayor," he told an appreciative audience. "They tell us business wouldn't go along. They're saying everybody would run out. They're saying city officials wouldn't cooperate. Well, Sears Tower ain't going nowhere. And neither is LaSalle Street or City Hall. No black could run this town? He couldn't do any worse than Jane Byrne!"[9]

The First District is a microcosm of black Chicago in many respects: it stretches from 31st Street south to 101st, across Grand Boulevard, Kenwood, Washington Park, Woodlawn, Grand Crossing, Chatham, and a dozen neighborhoods that have mirrored the rise of the black middle class and the despair of the black underclass. And it includes Hyde Park, the bastion of Southside independent politics and the one substantially integrated area in the territory. Black Chicago clearly resented the peculiar antics of the Byrne administration, and Washington, though running for Congress, was testing the waters in Chicago, trying to determine how deep that resentment went—whether it had the potential to awaken that elusive old Loch Ness monster, the black political power base.

It is by no means clear whether Washington, at that point in 1980, was envisioning the office of mayor for himself. Like other independents, he was trying to determine if the monster were myth

9

or reality. And the First District provided a most likely lagoon, because sightings of the monster had been reported there before. In 1972, backed by the Democratic organization for re-election as Cook County's state's attorney, Edward V. Hanrahan was devoured by an unexpected black outpouring—especially in the First District—with Washington leading that onslaught. In early 1976, when the organization tried to punish Metcalfe by slating Erwin France against him for Congress, the black power base arose again and gave the aging, ailing Metcalfe an incredible 70 percent majority. In 1978, after Metcalfe died, there was a surprise sighting. The organization stoutly refused Washington's demand for an open primary to find Metcalfe's successor, instead handing the nomination to party loyalist Stewart. In the general election, Republican Sammy Rayner, running as a protest alternative, garnered 40 percent of the popular vote in a district where genuine Republicans are as rare as the prehistoric auk.

The 1980 candidacy, then, can be regarded as Washington's critical test of voter discontent and of his own powers of persuasion. On both counts he came off with flying colors. He easily defeated his opponents, thanks to a huge turnout, and moved on to Washington, D.C., as a freshman congressman at the age of fifty-seven.

In that campaign Washington's poise under fire and his rhetorical skills drew considerable notice. There was an undeniable charisma about him: he was rugged, husky, macho-looking, with huge hands and broad shoulders. With his brow furrowed in concentration, he looked severe, almost menacing, like fullback Jim Brown about to blast into the enemy's line. But when he smiled, his whole face would light up with a jubilant kind of innocent pleasure, like a kid on the first day of summer vacation.

His command of words was growing legendary: Washington didn't avoid political deals, he "eschewed" them, just as he refuted old "canards," avoided embarrassing "contretemps," and wished his constituents peace and happiness in the "surcease" of their homes. He could quote knowledgeably from Shakespeare, Nietzsche, Abraham Lincoln, or the Bible, and, when the occasion demanded, he could with equal skill engage in down-home, funky banter with a group of welfare recipients or a class of black college students. Amazingly, he seemed sincere and secure in either role. His highfalutin phrases did not come across as snobbish, nor did his neighborhood jargon appear patronizing.

Besides that, Harold Washington had other powerful assets. He was an acknowledged workaholic who put in long hours on legislative matters; none of his associates could recall that he ever even took a vacation. He did not mingle with gamblers, underworld characters, narcotics dealers, or even with other politicians. He generally avoided parties and other social events. When he did come to one, he would sip from a glass of ginger ale. He dressed well though unpretentiously and lived modestly in a Southside apartment that was reportedly piled high with magazines, newspapers, and books (reporters were never invited in). His one occasional female companion was Mary Smith, a quiet Chicago schoolteacher who seemed to appear largely for ceremonial affairs—although she was to be identified later in the mayoral campaign as his fiancée.

In short, the dreams of those who had thought about a standard-bearer for black political empowerment began in 1980 to coalesce around Harold Washington. He seemed the sort of proven, capable, likable campaigner who just might snag that huge black vote and all of Chicago along with it. His only liability was the matter of the income tax, which—along with several other strange oversights—was to emerge with a vengeance in the heat of the mayoral campaign.

By almost any measure, politics was not a financially rewarding career for Washington. His finance reports between 1948 and 1979 showed him making usually less than $25,000 a year. His 1964 income as a lawyer, for example, was $8,999. Yet his very disregard for monetary rewards gave him an Achilles' heel.

In 1971, then Vice President Spiro Agnew, who was baiting liberals and "do-gooders," arrived in Springfield to address the state legislature. Washington publicly labeled him a phony and led a boycott of the speech. Soon afterwards, Washington was summoned by the Internal Revenue Service, which had noticed his failure to file any income tax returns from 1964 through 1967. Washington admitted guilt, claiming that he simply had overlooked filing, and subsequently served a month in Cook County Jail for the offenses. At the time, the transgression excited little voter notice and was covered only in back-page newspaper stories, partly because Washington was not yet a household name, partly because Chicago politicians were going to jail in considerable numbers, and partly because there was some suspicion that he had been unjustly targeted in retaliation for his independence.[10]

Washington's conviction was not a felony but a misdemeanor, as U.S. District Judge Joseph Sam Perry stated in the sentencing hearing: "I just want the record clear that this is not a fraud charge. This man is not charged with defrauding the government and filing false returns." Also, there was no accusation of any *attempt* to defraud the government. Taxes had been routinely deducted from Washington's salary as a state representative. He had, however, failed to file a statement for those four years. The federal audit found that he owed $35.33 for one year, $32.94 for the next, nothing for the third (he would have been eligible for a refund), and $439.58 for the fourth year. The grand total was $508.05.

According to some tax experts, the amounts owed in the case were so small that no criminal prosecution would have been brought if he had been an ordinary citizen. Yet, admittedly, Harold Washington was no ordinary citizen but one elected by his constituents to a position of public trust where the ethical demands should be higher than those for the public at large. Today the Criminal Tax Prosecution Code recommends action only if the evidence shows that the IRS may be able to retrieve $2,500 or more—about five times the amount Washington owed. At the hearing Judge Perry wondered why the government was descending so hard on one man when it was a well-known fact that other legislators in similar tax trouble had gotten "a free ride." The prosecutor indignantly denied that anyone ever got a free ride and claimed that Washington had actually failed to file for nineteen years! He offered no evidence to support the charge.

Two disturbing questions remained after the affair, questions which were to grow under cultivation by Republican mayoral candidate Bernard Epton into major issues. First, why didn't Washington file for the four years? "Stupidity," he said on one occasion. "That's all. You can't explain stupidity. It just happens. Hey, I'm no great hero whose life is perfectly consistent. Not at all. But I think I've shown that even a half-ass can do a lot of good if he puts some effort into it."[11] He just forgot, he said at other times, due to the pressure of his political and legal work. He and his lawyers flatly denied the nineteen-year allegation, claiming that they could have produced the appropriate tax returns if they had been compelled to.

Secondly, why didn't Washington fight the charges since the amounts were minuscule and other legislators, according to Judge Perry, were getting "free rides"? Political observers often cite that failure as Washington's biggest political mistake, and he has never commented on it in detail, except to imply that he viewed the government's charge as political persecution and feared falling into a deeper pit if he did not cooperate. To be sure, the Federal Bureau of Investigation had an extensive file of 500 entries detailing Washington's many civil rights activities. The Republican administration in Washington at the time was known to be moving against activists. Meanwhile, Mayor Richard Daley's organization in Chicago had a sizable list of anti-Washington grievances, including his role in the ouster of Hanrahan and his refusal to march with machine regulars in Springfield. He thus had little reason to anticipate anything resembling a free ride from either side. "He just wanted to get the stupid thing over with," reported one of his lawyers, "and get on with his life."[12]

In the mid-1970s Washington also incurred several substantial telephone and water bills that had not been settled even after the 1983 mayoral campaign was underway. The bills were for campaign office expenses during some of his hardest fights to hang onto his state legislative seat. That he had incurred these debts is no mystery, given his skimpy campaign war chest in those days. Why these old skeletons were not removed from the closet as soon as he won the 1983 Democratic mayoral primary (if not before) is a mystery.

There was also the matter of a single suspension of Washington's law license in the early 1970s for "failure to render adequate service." On several occasions, it was charged, he had accepted small sums from legal clients (between $15 and $60) and then did not follow through on the cases. He claimed the money represented down payments and that it was the clients who failed to pay the rest as agreed—a not uncommon situation for lawyers representing low-income clients. And he could have successfully defended himself in all probability before the disciplinary committee of the Chicago Bar Association—if he had only showed up for the hearing. Why he did not is another of the mysteries.

Then there was the old slum building which he and other relatives inherited from his father and for which taxes were long overdue. The recurring question is why he did not get rid of it, at least when he had every reason to believe that his opponent Epton would turn over every rock in his search for scandals.

The common denominator in all these gaffes appears to be a streak of sloppiness, especially in the affairs of his private life, combined with a certain naiveté. These characteristics are all the more intriguing because they are in marked contrast to Washington's well-cultivated and deserved image of a thoughtful, conscientious, reform-minded leader for whom no detail is too small. On the other hand, these failings by no means create the image of a sneaky, irresponsible criminal which his critics attempted to convey. If there is anything perfectly clear about Washington's record, it is that he had never used his office to benefit friends or enrich himself. And there is a certain irony in the fact that it was his blasé and careless attitude toward finance and favors that provoked the aura of scandal.

Back in the summer of 1982, little attention was paid to these matters, as the campaign to elect a black mayor was moving quietly but insistently forward. Among those in the forefront of the campaign were Lu Palmer, a former Chicago *Daily News* columnist and militant black power activist; Renault Robinson, director of the Afro-American Police League; Rev. Jesse Jackson, president of Operation PUSH; and Slim Coleman, leader of a racially mixed Northside political coalition called POWER. Palmer, in particular, had helped intensify among grass-roots black voters an antagonism toward Mayor Jane Byrne and a determination to put her out in 1983. And Byrne had cooperated with his campaign by consistently alienating the poor and the black—most notably in 1982 by replacing two black Chicago Housing Authority members with whites. This triggered the black boycott of the 1982 ChicagoFest and, more importantly, led to the registration of thousands of new black voters. A little-publicized Chicago Urban League study projected that by February 1983 blacks might well comprise 40 percent of the city's registered voters. If they were to vote as a bloc in a three-way Democratic primary, their candidate would easily win. And in a two-way general election, the black candidate would require only 11 percent of the white and Hispanic vote to achieve victory.

Based on Washington's popularity and his impressive First District Congressional win, Palmer, Robinson, and others considered him their first choice. And there were many intensive conferences with him on the subject. Reportedly, Washington was reluctant to throw his hat into the ring at first because he was fearful he would have to compete with a covey of other black hopefuls. But Robinson made the rounds, convincing all the likely candidates that it was in their interests to present a united front and get behind Harold Washington. If there was any dissent in the black community, it did not reach the ears of the press.

Washington agreed to run several months before he made the official announcement in early November, well aware that he was not on his own but part of an enthusiastic, mobilized campaign involving dozens of leaders and organizations. In effect, Washington, who inveighed against the Democratic machine, was the beneficiary and hand-picked choice of a peculiar little ad hoc machine assembled by assorted reformers and independents.

However, as he rode into the fray, he was careful not to make

Harold Washington, the first black to occupy the office of mayor in Chicago flashes the smile of a winner. When asked why he would even run against such formidable odds, Washington, a second generation public officeholder, said, "Politics is like shooting pool or eating Cracker Jacks. Once you start, you just can't stop." *(Office of the Mayor)*

An "enlightened" Republican legislator with a progressive voting record, Bernard E. Epton was forced by the circumstances of Chicago politics to play the role of representing disaffected neighborhoods and racial elements and consequently was put forth as a villain by liberals and a "racist" by the national news media. Had Jane Byrne won the primary, Epton would almost certainly have emerged as the darling of the lakefront liberals and the black community's "point man" to defeat the incumbent. Politics makes strange bedfellows. *(Epton campaign)*

Among the top female elected officials in the nation, Mayor Jane Byrne faced a formidable black political uprising in which black voters deserted the Democratic party's choice and voted for outside maverick Harold Washington. *(Office of the Mayor)*

Richard M. Daley, son of the late great boss, Richard J. Daley, was not an eloquent speaker but disproved those doubters who whispered that he could not stand on his feet and debate at the same time. Although "young Rich" put in a credible campaign and more than held his own in the debates, he ran last in every public opinion poll during the 1983 primary.   *(Holime)*

A part of the overflow crowd at Washington's huge Chicago Pavilion rally reflects some of the religio-political fervor that turned the campaign into a "black crusade." *(Chicago* Sun-Times)

In addition to his rugged, husky appearance, Washington is a capable debater with an amazing vocabulary who, legend has it, could wither a legislative foe in mid-argument. He could with equal ease engage in down-home, funky banter with welfare recipients or television newspersons. One observer predicted that no matter how he performs as mayor, the city's vocabulary is bound to expand. *(Al Cato)*

The ecstasy of victory on election night: State Senator Richard Newhouse (center) raises the hands of Harold Washington, Chicago's first black mayor, and his fiancée, Mary Smith. *(Chicago* Sun-Times)

Washington campaigned diligently in the city's huge black community. Seen here three days before the primary, Washington attracted a crowd at 22nd and State, one of Chicago's poorest neighborhoods. By this time Washington had become more than a black mayoral candidate and had attained the status of a black folk hero. *(Chicago* Sun-Times)

Even though he was the Democratic party's mayoral nominee, Washington was not given a high place of honor in the St. Patrick's parade. However, County Board President George Dunne, a bitter foe of Mayor Byrne, invited Harold Washington to march near the front of the parade. *(Al Cato)*

Elect
HAROLD
WASHINGTON
MAYOR

"I am running for mayor of Chicago because Jane Byrne is destroying this city....

—I believe that, together, you and I will make Chicago better for all of us."

Vote Feb. 22nd — Punch 9

Mayoral primary elections have historically pitted the "outs" and near "outs" against the "ins," and as Paul M. Green points out, the 1983 Washington's Birthday primary in Chicago brought an unexpected victory to near "out" Harold Washington. *(Holime)* any promises to his backers. He retained his characteristic independence. And he gave the impression that he was totally on his own, a knight errant taking on the dragons in City Hall. "Don't let anyone whisper that a black can't run this city," he bellowed in a typical campaign speech. "I can run the hell out of this city. I've spent the last two years dealing with budgets of 200-odd billions of dollars. You mean to tell me you don't think I can handle a budget of $2 billion? Don't let anybody tell you I can't run this city!"[13]

The Washington campaign organization underwent numerous behind-the-scenes changes and was at times on the verge of collapse. In public, however, the congressman maintained an air of cool, detached confidence and discovered, he admitted, "levels of energy I didn't know I had," as he worked daily from 6:00 a.m. to midnight making appearances and stirring up the crowds. His campaign promises—economic development, power to the neighborhoods, fair treatment for women and minorities, and government efficiency—were all issues he had supported both in Springfield and Washington. And so his platform had a genuine consistency.

Gradually, the campaign assumed crusade proportions and might have become an overwhelming juggernaut were it not for the stream of disclosures about the unpaid bills and the license suspension and the income tax matter. Consistently, Washington's strategy was to treat these failings as trivial—an approach that alienated many white voters who had been sitting on the fence. When *Sun-Times* columnist Mike Royko sniped at him for failing to face these past transgressions, Washington said, "Royko runs hot and cold. He's no benchmark of intelligent political thought for me."[14]

A few weeks before the election, a newsman asked Al Raby, the embattled campaign manager, how he and others on the firing line were weathering the storm. "Fine," he said. "How often do you get the chance to work with a man who is a giant, who has such warmth, confidence, and charisma, a man who embodies the political aspirations of a people? How much more could anyone ask for?"[15]

On election day it became clear that thousands of Chicago voters shared that assessment. The disclosures hurt, to be sure, but they did not prove fatal because, at least in the black community, Harold Washington had assumed the status of a folk hero. He was obviously enjoying this storybook climax to his unorthodox political career when he told the cheering audience at his campaign headquarters, "You want Harold? Well, you got him!"

1. Telephone interview with 3rd Ward precinct captain, April 13, 1983.
2. Harold Washington campaign speech, February 13, 1983.
3. Quoted in the Chicago *Sun-Times,* April 10, 1983.
4. Bennett Johnson, quoted in Chicago *Sun-Times,* April 10, 1983.
5. Interview with Harold Washington, January 20, 1980.
6. Cited by David Moberg, Chicago *Reader,* February 11, 1983.
7. *Chicago* magazine, November 1977; Chicago *Sun-Times,* December 10, 1977.
8. Quoted in Chicago *Reader,* February 11, 1983.
9. Interview with Harold Washington, January 20, 1983.
10. Yet the suspicions of conspiracy nursed by Washington partisans are weakened by the strange turn of events which two years later saw the IRS come down hard on Agnew and drive him from the vice presidency.
11. Interview with Harold Washington, June 8, 1976.
12. Lawrence Kennon, quoted in Chicago *Reader,* April 8, 1983.
13. Quoted in Chicago *Reader,* February 11, 1983.
14. Quoted in Chicago *Reader,* February 11, 1983.
15. Interview with Al Raby, February 28, 1983.

II

The Primary: Some New Players —Same Old Rules

PAUL M. GREEN

"Race was key in this campaign, for it would not be difficult to argue that if Harold Washington were white he would not have entered, let alone won, the 1983 Chicago Democratic mayoral primary."

—Paul M. Green

In the mid-1930s, Chicago Alderman Robert Jackson, a black Republican from the city's 3rd Ward, exhorted his black audience to support black congressional candidate William Dawson. Jackson said, "We must stick together to get somewhere as a race. Every Jew will hunt and vote for a Jew. The same for the Irish and every other race. The Negro can't find a Negro's name to save his life. Look for his name until you find it. He's your own flesh and blood and nobody is going to vote for him if you don't."[1] Some fifty years later Chicago's black voters heeded similar "flesh and blood" pleas and supported black Congressman Harold Washington for the Democratic mayoral nomination. On February 22, 1983, black Chicagoans hunted, found, and voted for Washington in such numbers that they defeated both incumbent Mayor Jane Byrne and Cook County State's Attorney Richard M. Daley in the most expensive campaign in the city's history.

I. THE CHICAGO MAYORAL PRIMARY: AN HISTORICAL BACKGROUND

An overlooked measuring stick of city politics in general and Chicago politics in particular is how party leaders and members have selected their candidates for the city's top political prize—the mayor's office. Often the struggles inside the party have reflected the city's

17

political atmosphere more clearly than have general mayoral elections or any other political contest. No other single political indicator informs us more accurately on the development of party organization, the aspirations and ascendancy of the city's ethnic groups, or the voters' gut views on key issues than do Chicago's mayoral primaries. Overall, the hotly contested 1983 Chicago Democratic mayoral primary was not dramatically dissimilar to previous internal party battles.

Starting in 1879, when Chicagoans elected Democrat Carter Harrison I, the city's first modern mayor, Chicago's politics as expressed in its party selection process has undergone four distinct political periods. From 1879 to 1915, personality politics dominated the political scene. Under Harrison and his son, Carter Harrison II— each elected five times to City Hall—Chicago politics was made up of myriad shifting factional alliances based on ethnicity and neighborhood. Loyalty was given to individuals who acted like "wardlords" in controlling their isolated ethnic or neighborhood enclaves.

Attempts to build citywide organizations in both parties failed because local leaders shifted their allegiances and party factions engaged in legendary cutthroat political "knifing" battles, which became known in Chicago as "rule or ruin" politics. In this situation, a party faction defeated in a mayoral primary or convention would covertly or openly throw its support to the opposition party candidate to prevent an intraparty rival faction from gaining City Hall political patronage.

A second political period, from 1915 to 1933, reveals the mayoral primary system being used differently by Chicago's two major parties. During this period Chicago Republicans controlled City Hall for twelve years under the mercurial and controversial leadership of William Hale "Big Bill" Thompson, the city's last GOP mayor. Thompson ripped apart the fabric of Republican support in the city by personalizing party control and making city GOP political fortunes totally intertwined with his own flamboyant career. His close association with noted underworld figures, his questionable administrative tactics, and his outlandish political behavior made voting Democratic more acceptable to a great cross section of Chicago's electorate.

Unlike their Republican counterparts, Chicago's Democrats were pulling their party together during the period between 1915 and 1933. As the old factional leaders died off, they were replaced by so-called "new breed Democrats"[2] who were better educated and more willing to organize themselves into a citywide coalition. Leading the "new breed movement" was Anton Cermak, who brilliantly parlayed this desire for party unity with the political mobilization movement of thousands of new ethnic voters. Under his leadership these two new political realities gave birth to an all-encompassing multinationality political organization, or machine.

The third period stretches from 1933 to 1976, and it is the golden period of machine politics Chicago style. Only three mayoral primaries took place during this period: the first two, in 1939 and 1955, were battles for party leadership, while the last one, in 1975, reflected real organizational decline and the growth of political reform pressure in the city. During this period (which starts with the assassination of Mayor Cermak) only three men resided in City Hall: under Ed Kelly the Democratic organization rambled; it stalled slightly under the lukewarm reform leadership of Martin Kennelley; and it accelerated into overdrive under the dynamic direction of Richard J. Daley.

When the political dust settled during the glory days of Daley's reign, several important facts became clearly visible. The Republican party had been eliminated organizationally and politically in Chicago. The growing number of city black residents who had trickled slowly into the Democratic party during the 1930s and 1940s had become a tidal wave of new Democratic voters during the 1950s and 1960s. Lastly, old neighborhood ethnic Democratic voters had pushed outward from the city center to its periphery, thereby turning once staunch, hardcore GOP communities into heavy turnout Democratic wards. Furthermore, these new ethnic middle- and upper-middle-class areas became the breeding grounds for its future party leaders.

Daley's political goal was to replace individual loyalty to a faction, a person, a nationality, or a neighborhood with unstinting loyalty to an organization. Late in his life, this complicated and often brilliant man saw his Democratic organization cracking at the edges. A perpetually weak and often tolerated lakeshore independent reform movement found a new and potentially powerful ally in the emerging black middle class located on the city's far South Side. In the 1975 Democratic mayoral primary—Daley's last real campaign—both movements found leaders willing to take on Daley and his organization. Alderman William Singer, a forceful lakefront independent, garnered 29 percent of the primary vote, carried two wards, and received over 40 percent of the vote in six Northside wards. Richard Newhouse, a black state senator, gained only 8 percent of the vote; but in four black middle-class wards he received over

20 percent of the vote. Daley's death in 1976 ended the career of the nation's last true political boss, but it is unlikely that the changes taking place inside the Democratic party would have slowed greatly even if he had continued on as mayor.

Since Mayor Daley's death in December 1976, Chicago primary politics has entered its fourth period of development. There have been as many contested mayoral primaries since Daley's departure as there were in the previous forty-three years. Without question, the once omnipotent political machine has sputtered, as political characteristics that prevailed before Cermak's organizational consolidation have returned to Chicago politics. Currently one can observe increased ward regionalism, recurring organization breakdowns in key campaigns, politically unyielding racial and ethnic pride, an ongoing lack of party leadership, and the return of factional alliances.

Further contributing to organization decay was the addition of another dissident group. The ethnic voters from Chicago's heavily Polish Northwest Side broke machine ranks in the special 1977 mayoral primary (called following Daley's death) to support 41st Ward Alderman Roman Pucinski. In 1977 Pucinski, a Northwest Side spokesman, challenged the organization candidate Michael Bilandic in a wide-open primary. The alderman won 33 percent of the primary vote, carried seven wards, and received at least 40 percent of the vote in fourteen mainly Northwest Side wards. Also running in the primary was Harold Washington, then an Illinois state legislator, who captured 11 percent of the vote, won five wards, and received 30 percent of the vote in twelve black wards.

Two years later, Jane Byrne challenged Bilandic one-on-one and beat the incumbent mayor in the now-famous snow-filled primary. The key to Byrne's win, outside of the elements, was the coalescing of existing antiorganization forces behind her candidacy. Byrne won twenty-nine wards in three main areas of the city (the middle-class black South Side, the string of lakefront independent/ liberal wards, and several wards in Chicago's Northwest Side Polish community). Her later reconciliation with the organization did not dilute the fact that potent political forces were working in the Chicago electorate and from the traditional machine's viewpoint, "they were out of control." Thus, as 1983 rolled around, it was not surprising that the organization would be challenged; the only question was by whom and how many. Once again, Chicago's mayoral primary would serve as a vehicle by which the "outs" and "near outs" would confront the "ins" for city control.

II. 1983 DEMOCRATIC MAYORAL PRIMARY: THE COMBATANTS

Few local campaigns in this country, indeed in the world, have ever generated such sustained intensity as Chicago's 1983 Democratic mayoral primary. In a city where politics is king, this eventual three-way contest was the ultimate battle royal. The incumbent mayor was Jane Byrne. She had been the surprise antiorganization victor in a weather-inspired mayoral primary four years earlier. (She was actually elected mayor when she defeated Republican Wallace Johnson in the general mayoral election following the primary, but in recent decades that legal mayoral requirement had been reduced to a minor political formality.)

Once in office as the city's first woman mayor, Byrne patched up her differences with the machine and embarked on a fund-raising program unmatched in the city's history. She also gave Chicago an administration that reflected her own feisty personality. A notorious political hipshooter, Byrne's record contained both spectacular hits and many well-publicized misses. A former protégée of the late Mayor Richard J. Daley, Byrne sought to recapture overnight the political power and personal magic that had taken her mentor a lifetime to build.

It was Mayor Daley's eldest son, Richard, who emerged as the major political obstacle to her dream. Young Daley had been a rather unspectacular state senator when Byrne took over City Hall, but soon he was forced by Byrne to either capitulate to her demands for citywide political domination or take her on for control of both the city and the party. In late 1979 Daley accepted the challenge by announcing his candidacy for Cook County state's attorney. As the boy from Bridgeport, an old working-class neighborhood on Chicago's near Southwest Side, Daley had had little exposure in the rest of the city or its surrounding suburbs. But a year later, after beating Byrne-backed opponents in the primary and general election, Richard M. Daley became state's attorney and a real force in Chicago politics, as well as a rallying symbol for those eager to dump Byrne in 1983.

The intense anti-Byrne fervor of Rich Daley's supporters keyed his primary organization strategy. To diehard Daleyites, this campaign was not just mayoral politics—it was political restoration. Their laundry list of Byrne's economic and administrative blunders barely covered their underlying emotional zeal to purge her from City Hall. Not only had she openly attempted to snuff out young

Daley's political career (in Chicago, the sons of famous political leaders have "young" preceding their names until they die or have politically active children of their own), but when given the opportunity, she snubbed Daley's Southwest Side bailiwick, his political supporters, and worst of all, Mrs. Richard J. Daley, the late mayor's well-respected widow. Daley's legions wanted war, and they made no provision for taking any political prisoners.

The third major Democratic primary challenger was First District black congressman Harold Washington. A former state legislator and machine stalwart, Washington's gradual shift to political independence reflected the growth of the city's black middle class. In 1977 his ill-financed and poorly organized mayoral primary run had netted him five wards and 11 percent of the vote. An erudite and articulate campaigner, Washington was more adept speaking before well-educated, middle-class audiences than he was stumping before less-informed and economically disadvantaged voters. Complicating his political posture was his 1972 jail term on his conviction for failing to file federal income tax returns. Few political experts doubted that this issue would be exploited in white city neighborhoods; the big question was what impact it would have in Chicago's burgeoning black wards.

III. OPENING SKIRMISHES

The first blood in the 1983 mayoral primary battle was drawn nearly one year before the actual contest when 10th Ward Alderman Edward Vrdolyak replaced Cook County Board President George Dunne as chairman of the Cook County Democratic Central Committee. Mayor Byrne was concerned about Dunne's loyalty during her renomination bid, and in March 1982 she engineered a coup to topple Dunne from the powerful committee chairmanship. The mayor saw Vrdolyak, a hard-nosed political infighter from the city's far Southeast Side steel mill area, as a tough and articulate point man who could handle the expected frontal assault from the Daley forces. In the 1983 mayoral primary Daley would receive the endorsements of eleven of the fifty ward committeemen. Interestingly, ten of the eleven supported Dunne against Vrdolyak in the chairmanship battle. For the record, the only Vrdolyak supporter who endorsed Daley for mayor was Congressman Dan Rostenkowski.

The next pre-primary salvo was fired in June at the Democratic national mini-convention in Philadelphia. Two Daley allies, Cook County Assessor Thomas Hynes and the state's attorney's brother

Bill, accused the mayor of breaking her promises by raising taxes, of politicizing city government, and for employing "a come up and see me some time approach to (urban) planning."[3] Byrne, angered at the sneak attack, shot back that Daley and Hynes had mounted an insidious campaign against her which she labeled "a form of deception." The mayor claimed that Daley and his entire family had been running against her since the day she walked in the door. She said the state's attorney was hiding behind the assessor and Bill Daley because he could not take the heat of press conferences, interviews, or open debate. Lastly, she countered on the volatile tax increase issue by revealing a political tactic that would grow into the keystone of her renomination strategy. According to Byrne, the city was in such surprisingly bad economic shape when she took office in 1979 that any blame for needed tax increases should be placed on her City Hall predecessors.

Sporadic political sniping between the Byrne and Daley camps followed the Philadelphia skirmish, but most political pundits believed that the mayoral combatants would call a temporary ceasefire as the upcoming statewide elections grew imminent. However, in July, Mayor Byrne once again confounded and dazzled foes and friends alike by replacing two black members of the Chicago Housing Authority (CHA) with two whites. Precipitating this move had been the mayor's all-out effort to save the reputation of her white housing board chairman and chief fund-raiser, Charles Swibel, whom she also replaced with another white, Andrew J. Mooney. Byrne's maneuver gave whites a majority on the CHA Board in a city where 84 percent of the 142,000 public housing tenants were black. The mayor justified her action by stating that the three new board members had "managerial expertise needed to reform the troubled, deficit-ridden agency."[4] Insiders discounted her public explanation by claiming that Byrne was goading her black critics into putting up a black candidate in the Democratic primary in the belief that she could split her enemy Daley's support. In a city where "hardball politics" is considered routine, it seemed as if Byrne had gone out of her way to inflame Chicago's black voters. Many observers were astonished.

A number of Chicago's black leaders, led by Rev. Jesse Jackson, reacted swiftly to Byrne's blatant political slap in the face. They hastily organized a black boycott of the mayor's August ChicagoFest—a twelve-day festival featuring topflight entertainment and ethnic food. More important, they began a major voter registration drive in the black community and plastered the slogan "come alive on October 5" (the last day for registration) on bill-boards and storefronts. For the first time in Chicago history, new black voters outnumbered new white voters. In the seventeen pre-dominantly black wards registration activity was frenzied. This black political reaction erupted on election day, November 2, 1982, when Chicago's black voters nearly stopped Republican Governor James R. Thompson's third-term bid by giving county and state Democratic candidates overwhelming vote totals in their wards. The black surge was genuine and powerful, and First District black Congressman Harold Washington suddenly found himself being squeezed to lead a black crusade against the machine.

IV. WAR IS DECLARED

Two days after the November general election, Richard M. Daley officially announced his candidacy for the Democratic mayoral nomination. Even the fuss and fury arising from the razor-thin guber-natorial contest was pushed off center stage by Daley's declaration. *Sun-Times* columnist Mike Royko gleefully proclaimed: ". . . for many Chicagoans the preliminary skirmishing is over. . . . Choosing a governor . . . can be entertaining but now we get down to the serious war—the election of a mayor."[5]

Daley attacked the "current administration" (he never men-tioned Byrne's name) for raising taxes, mismanagement, and inef-fective leadership. His infant candidacy received a major boost when 45th Ward Democratic Committeeman Thomas Lyons from the city's far Northwest Side threw his organization behind Daley. Over-looked in the euphoria surrounding Daley's announcement, how-ever, was his top strategists' assertion that the first two months of the campaign would be devoted to assembling an organization and fund-raising. Daley's decision not to immediately blitz Byrne with a hard-hitting media campaign would prove to be a fatal flaw in his mayoral bid.

Less than a week after Daley's announcement, Congressman Washington entered the Democratic mayoral primary field. He had received enormous pressure from black political and community leaders to enter the race. Throughout September and October he hedged on making a final decision, but the staggering and unprec-edented new black voter registrations convinced him of the viability of a black candidacy. Aiding his decision was the realization that if he did not carry the standard, another black candidate would be found to lead an existing, genuine, ongoing political movement.

Washington's November 1982 announcement of his mayoral candidacy was highlighted by his accusations that "the city that supposedly works, doesn't" and that "Chicago is a city divided . . . where citizens are treated unequally and unfairly. . . ."[6] He also asserted that his 1972 legal problems were behind him and that his life was "as open as anyone else's."[7] Finally, the Congressman claimed that the current energized black political situation had converted him from a reluctant candidate to one who would campaign with gusto. Washington prophetically argued that the masses of white people would split between Daley and Byrne, thereby enhancing the chances of a black candidate.

On November 22, one day before the city Democratic ward committeemen would endorse their candidates, Byrne officially announced her re-election bid. For several months previous to that, the mayor had undergone a remarkable political and personal metamorphosis. Under the guidance of New York media adviser David Sawyer, she had toned down her demeanor, her dress, and her rhetoric. The new Jane Byrne was cool and professional, and she stressed her administrative competence by reiterating her charge that she brought the city back from imminent financial disaster in 1979. Moreover, in a series of shrewd and lightning-fast political moves, which included a $50 million one-shot influx of new revenue from the sale of bonds for an O'Hare Airport expansion, she was able to offer Chicagoans a $30 million package of tax relief.

V. DEMOCRATIC SLATEMAKING

Political slatemaking in Chicago is a throwback to the days when politics required guts, nerve, and wit instead of media advisers and computers. In a tension-filled room in the basement of the Bismarck Hotel on November 23, 1982, Democratic ward committeemen met to finish off the first round of the campaign by endorsing a mayoral candidate. Besides their political importance and dramatic intrigue, slatemaking sessions provide the best evidence concerning the condition of the Chicago Democratic organization. Following this session, no one could doubt that the party organization was split wide open.

The rituals of Democratic slatemaking in Chicago are legendary. Like a giant group of salmon swimming upstream, party leaders gravitate to the session. Prior to the call to order, political "has beens" and "never beens" mingle with real power brokers, conversing in whispers and recognizing each other with a nod or a tug of the coat sleeve. Those not privileged to have a reserved seat fight for a prominent place along the front wall where they can see and hear speaker and audience without interference. Everybody looks like he knows the inside story, but he will share it only with a trusted friend or a potential political ally.

A rush of aldermen arrives, many of them ward committeemen, and the historic meeting suddenly begins. Nowhere in American politics is there such a devotion to traditional hierarchical structure or tribalism as in this meeting. The Irish clan philosophy survives even if the Irish no longer dominate the committee. Everybody in the room longs to sit in one of the sacred fifty ward committeeman chairs. But all are somewhat befuddled by the actions of 27th Ward Committeeman Edward Quigley, the head of the sewer department. Not once during the meeting does Quigley sit down or turn his back on the audience; instead, he eyeballs spectators and committeemen alike, peering intently at every face in the crowd.

From the outset of the meeting Chairman Vrdolyak is clearly in command, even though he turns the gavel over to 47th Ward Committeeman and Park District Superintendent Ed Kelly. Byrne's endorsement has been carefully orchestrated, and Her Honor's brief speech goes well as she humbly presents herself before the committee. She chides Daley and Washington for refusing to go after the endorsement, and she remains at the head table to hear committeeman after committeeman praise her job performance and her gutsy personality. Most of the pro-Byrne speeches are repetitious and predictable, but finally Vrdolyak lays out the political bottom line for the next three months. In a clear and confident voice he tells the committeemen, "Chicago needs Jane Byrne," and "if anyone wants to take us [the Democratic organization] on, they better pack a lunch because it will be an all-day job."

Vrdolyak's speech is followed by a motion by his trusted lieutenant, 14th Ward Committeeman Ed Burke, that calls for a unanimous endorsement of Jane Byrne for mayor. After some wrangling, former County Chairman George Dunne stands up, looks Byrne straight in the eye, and demands that his vote be recorded as "no" on her endorsement. The issue is joined, and any hope for unity has been scuttled. For the next ten minutes the smartest and toughest Chicago politicians go at each other openly.

Dunne's dramatic move is followed by a series of procedural questions concerning the endorsement process. Daniel Rostenkowski, chairman of the powerful U.S. House Ways and Means Committee—but for this event more importantly 32nd Ward committeeman—leads the questioning of the chair's endorsing process. Instinctively, Vrdolyak pushes Kelly away from the microphone as he and Rostenkowski go head to head with little interruption. The room, which had been noisy throughout the meeting, is now completely silent. If an atom bomb were to fall on State Street and Madison Avenue at that moment, no spectator would leave the confrontation. Eventually, an endorsement roll call is taken, and twelve more committeemen join Dunne in refusing to support Byrne. The mayor walks away with a battle victory, but even her most ardent backers recognize that the war has just begun. Daley and Washington committeemen have held firm, and they are ready to challenge Byrne and the existing Democratic organization for city control.

VI. BYRNE ON THE ATTACK

The political momentum in the early weeks of the primary campaign clearly belonged to Mayor Byrne. With all the advantages of incumbency, a multimillion-dollar war chest, and a strong alliance with Chairman Vrdolyak, she seemed way ahead of both her opponents. Chicagoans saw on television and heard on radio the Byrne message that yes, she had made some mistakes, but that she had learned her job so well that today Chicago was in better fiscal shape than any other major northern city. The new Byrne claimed that she was still tough and feisty, but that was what it took to run a town as tough as Chicago. Byrne's early bombardment truly shook Daley's strategists, who had underestimated the power of her saturation campaign on the airwaves.

Byrne was also aided during this early period by the stumbles of the barely assembled Daley and Washington campaign staffs. The state's attorney foundered for nearly six weeks before accepting the challenge to debate his opponents. Daley's reluctance to meet Byrne and Washington head-on reinforced charges that he was inarticulate and unable to think on his feet. It put Daley on the defensive and turned attention away from his attempt to focus the campaign on the mayor's record. Washington's campaign lacked organization, money, and direction, and the candidate lurched about looking for the kinds of themes that would attract new supporters and campaign contributors. The low point of the Washington campaign came on Christmas Day, when the congressman, escorted by Rev. Jackson, visited Cook County Jail. TV cameras recorded the appearance, and on Christmas night Chicagoans saw a black candidate holding a rally before a large group of mainly black inmates. Don Rose, a leading "independent" political strategist, called the visit "the biggest campaign boner of the season," adding "that it [upset] more blacks than whites."

The new year found Byrne still on the offensive and her two opponents trying to react to her various political moves. On New Year's Eve the mayor treated thousands of Chicagoans to free fireworks displays across the city. She refused to fall back into the old Jane Byrne mold when she decided to retain respected cable TV adviser John McGuire after a clumsy effort to replace him with a party hack. The mayor and Vrdolyak then demonstrated the payoff for party defection by engineering a board revolt against County Board President Dunne that stripped him of most of his considerable powers. Finally, Byrne transferred $10 million that had been budgeted for street improvements and set up a temporary job program for 3,800 unemployed Chicagoans. Byrne's maneuvers were so deft that they partially eclipsed the endorsements Daley was garnering from lakefront independents like State Senator Dawn Clark Netsch and Alderman Martin Oberman, as well as the series of thoughtful position papers Daley issued on improving city finances and services. As for Washington, his campaign also picked up a bit under its new chairman, former civil rights leader Al Raby. The congressman also laid to rest many doubts about his previous income tax troubles with a fine speech before the Rotary Club in downtown Chicago.

VII. DEBATES AND ENDORSEMENTS

In late January the Chicago mayoral campaign centered on a series of four debates during a two-week period. Not surprisingly, in the aftermath all three candidates expressed happiness with their respective performances during the sometimes rancorous face-to-face confrontations. Byrne could rightfully point out that under excruciating political pressure she had kept her cool, defended her record against two challengers, and leveled a few barbs of her own at both foes. Daley surprised many people with his competence, knowledge, and sense of humor (especially after the first debate), and few questioned his victory in the third debate, when he ripped into Byrne and her media adviser, Sawyer. But the big debate winner was Washington, who in the widely publicized and observed first debate showed voters—especially black voters—that he was an articulate and legitimate candidate.

Though the debates boosted Washington's political fortunes

and made him a viable candidate, they did not make him the eventual primary winner. Rather, it was to be political developments totally outside Washington's control that influenced and redistributed support among anti-Washington voters that cut the final returns in the congressman's favor. On January 23, *one month before the election,* the Chicago *Tribune* endorsed Daley, calling him "the best hope." Ten days later, the *Sun-Times* did the same, claiming that the state's attorney had "a reputation for reliability and integrity." Highlighting both major newspapers' editorial moves was not only the unprecedented endorsement swiftness but the preview of how they were going to treat Mayor Byrne for the rest of the primary campaign.

For many it seemed that both newspapers' editorials were more anti-Byrne than pro-Daley. Yet for the beleaguered state's attorney's campaign the endorsements and subsequent positive press coverage was perfectly timed political adrenalin. Despite a better-than-expected debate performance, Daley's primary campaign was at a low ebb. Polls showed that voters believed Byrne to be the more competent administrator, and her strength was growing among the so-called "thinking voters" along the lakefront and the Northwest Side. The newspaper endorsements boosted Daley's image, revitalized his workers' spirits, and put him back in the political ballgame. In addition, the newspapers' savage and nearly continuous attacks on Byrne tore away her support in those areas where she had to build substantial margins. In the end, the break in Byrne's late January political momentum, caused in large part by newspaper criticism, evened up white support for her and Daley along the lake and on the Northwest Side and allowed Washington to gain the campaign initiative.

VIII. THE FINAL FEBRUARY PUSH

The final three weeks of the campaign was an old-fashioned Chicago free-for-all. No high-stakes poker players ever put more chips on the table than did the three Democratic mayoral candidates. Charges flew between the camps, with the sharpest exchanges taking place between the Daley and Byrne forces. Political endorsements came in from all over, as national, state, and local leaders sided with one of the three candidates. On the streets workers battled each other for poster space on windows, sides of buildings, and lampposts. No Chicago neighborhood was left unvisited. Local television added to the intensity by inundating viewers with political news. No other story anywhere in the world could have interested Chicagoans more than this primary battle, and the city's print and electronic media gave its citizens what they wanted: "nonstop politics."

Each of the candidates employed a different strategy in the campaign's closing days. Daley was the attacker. He accused Byrne of trying to buy the election with a $10 million campaign fund; he ridiculed her use of outside consultants; and, with the help of Mike Royko and the *Sun-Times,* he hammered away at the ethics of the mayor's closest aides. To win, Daley needed a 100,000-vote plurality on the Southwest Side, significant ward victories on the Northwest and North sides, and whatever he could get in the black wards. As these goals began to appear possible, Daley's staff worried most about the impact of published newspaper and TV polls showing him trailing both Byrne and Washington. Daley claimed that Chicagoans were afraid to tell the truth to telephone pollsters and that his own straw polls (which he mass-distributed attached to an open letter from Senator Netsch that substantiated the accuracy of past Daley straw polls) showed him in the lead and picking up momentum. Nevertheless, on the Friday before the election, both newspaper and media polls found Daley still in third place, which generated a series of events that one Daley aide called the politics of "the lost weekend."

For much of the last part of the campaign Mayor Byrne was the defender. Her once enormous lead in the polls had dwindled as both Washington and Daley gained ground. Announcements such as federal approval for a rapid transit link to Midway Airport or the completion of the Chicago Transit Authority's extension to O'Hare Airport hardly slowed down the speed with which the gap was closing. Desperate for an issue on which to take the offensive and deflect the daily shellacking she was receiving in the press, the mayor claimed that she was being picked on because she was a female. She appealed to Chicago's women voters, especially black women, by saying, "It's tough to have two men bootin' your head every day."[8] But it was the race issue and the fear of a Washington victory that energized Byrne's campaign in the final days. Led by Chairman Vrdolyak, the Democratic organization parlayed the latest poll results into an all-out effort to turn the campaign into a two-way race. In a now famous incident, Vrdolyak apparently told a Northwest Side precinct rally "that a vote for Daley is a vote for Washington" and that the campaign had become "a racial thing . . . [because] we're fighting to keep the city the way it is."[9] Though Vrdolyak vigorously denied ever making the statement, evidence suggests that he and other Byrne supporters set up an elaborate phone bank to warn white Chicagoans of a possible Washington victory. Thousands of Chicago voters received weekend phone calls urging them not to throw away their vote on Daley but to support Byrne as the best hope of keeping Washington out of City Hall.

While Daley and Byrne cut each other apart, Washington closed his campaign running like a winner. A massive rally, held in the new Chicago Pavilion at the University of Illinois in Chicago and attended by over 12,000 people two weeks before the election, had ignited his campaign by turning his candidacy into a black crusade. Washington solidified his support in the black community with little loss to Daley and only sporadic gains by Byrne. Days before the election, the congressman claimed that he had the contest won and that only massive vote theft could deny him a primary victory. Washington's confidence was based on an "80-80" political strategy: an 80 percent black turnout, and an 80 percent share of that vote. In vote percentages, the "80-80 strategy" would give Washington 40 percent of the Democratic primary vote cast. Thus, the only way he could lose was if either Daley or Byrne annihilated the other in the white wards. In the campaign's closing hours, Washington fostered the Daley-Byrne competition by claiming that "you can put a sheet of paper between the two of them."[10]

IX. HOW WASHINGTON WON—THE RETURNS

On February 22nd, 1,235,324—or 77.5 percent—of Chicago's eligible voters went to the polls, and 98.6 percent of those voting asked for a Democratic ballot. Democratic applications for ballots in the 1983 Democratic mayoral primary totaled almost 400,000 more than the hotly contested Byrne-Bilandic primary in 1979.

How did the wards line up in 1983? Ten wards turned out 80 percent or more of their voters, but none of these were pro-Washington black wards; they were white ethnic wards on the Northwest and Southwest sides. Washington's goal of 80 percent turnout in the city's sixteen predominantly black wards fell short: these wards averaged a 73 percent turnout. Nevertheless, the huge increase in the number of new black registrations and the significant solid Washington turnout in these communities, coupled with scattered pockets of black, white, and Latino support in other parts of Chicago, gave Washington the raw numbers to surpass Byrne and Daley.

Although Washington was unsuccessful in turning out 80 percent of the black vote, he had little problem in convincing

80 percent of those blacks voting to vote for him. All but two of Washington's ward victories were in almost solid black wards, and they were all landslides. In fact, twenty-one wards citywide were won by one of the candidates with 60 percent or more of the vote. Of those twenty-one wards, Washington had seventeen, Daley had three, while Byrne had only one. In terms of pluralities, Washington's black wards out-produced long-time white ethnic enclaves throughout the city. Because Daley and Byrne generally split the white vote, while Washington had a relatively free ride in black areas, Washington's margins were prodigious where he won. Incredibly, Washington received higher vote margins in five black wards than Daley received from his family's legendary 11th Ward fiefdom.

A precinct analysis of Chicago's 2,914 precincts reveals the undeniable racial voting patterns and the closeness of the contest. Byrne and Washington were nearly even in precincts won, both doubling Daley's total of precinct victories. In all-black wards Washington's precinct returns were awesome: in ten black wards he won every precinct, mainly by lopsided margins, while Byrne and Daley had only one ward apiece where neither of their opponents carried a precinct.[11]

Key to Washington's victory was that he rode the race issue in wards that contained only a small number of black voters. In these mainly white-dominated wards, organization endorsements and ward committeeman loyalty meant nothing as black precincts overwhelmingly supported Washington. It is a certainty that many black political jobholders went against their sponsors' wishes and voted race over organization.

Election night was largely a great disappointment for State's Attorney Daley. He won only nine city wards, and by margins far less than he and his advisers had thought possible. He carried his Southwest Side bailiwick by only a bit over half of his hoped-for 100,000-margin, and he even ended up losing the neighboring 14th and 15th wards. Except for the wards of his long-time allies, Cook County Assessor Hynes (19th) and Congressman William Lipinski (23rd), no other ward outside of his own 11th gave Daley more than 60 percent of their vote. On the other hand, he performed well in certain Northwest and North Side wards, where he battled the mayor and her committeemen to virtual standstills. But Daley was destroyed in the black community: he was unable to win more than 10 percent of the vote in fifteen black wards (Washington was also unable to win 10 percent of the votes in fifteen white wards). Daley stalwarts will for years to come blame Vrdolyak, Byrne, and their henchmen for sandbagging their candidate during the last weekend of the campaign as they reconsider the big question: "Did Richie have the votes to win on the Friday before the election?"

Mayor Byrne carried more wards—twenty-one—than did either of her opponents. She also had only two wards, Daley's 11th and the middle-class black 21st, where she received less than 10 percent of a ward's vote. But she had only one ward, Alderman Richard Mell's 33rd, where she recieved 60 percent of the vote. Byrne's inability to produce a few large-margin ward victories and her poor showing in the black community caused her defeat. Even her better than expected totals against Daley on the Southwest Side could not offset her dropoffs in the black wards. In the three-way race, Byrne was cutting into the strength of the wrong candidate in the campaign's waning hours. Inside speculation suggests that Vrdolyak's dramatic moves on the last weekend truly hurt Daley, but at the same time it solidified black support for Washington. Thus, on election day, Byrne's final surge did not take many votes, if any, from the candidate in the lead—Harold Washington.

Another shock for Byrne was her disappointing performance in the lakefront and Northwest Side wards. Despite nearly unanimous ward organization support, the mayor could only just beat Daley in areas where she needed to demolish him. With a few exceptions, Byrne fell victim to a resurgent distrust of her mayoral record among North Side residents who had positively reassessed her performance in January 1983, only to reverse their position once again a month later.

At Byrne headquarters on election night, one worker whimsically summed up the mayor's defeat: "Well, that's the way the cabal bounces." Most of Byrne's supporters, however, were shocked and mystified by Washington's victory over their candidate. Indeed, it is somewhat hard to believe that after four years in office and the expenditure of millions of campaign dollars, Chicago's first woman mayor had frittered away the good will and special feelings she had captured in her brilliant 1979 victories. Her dreams of a political dynasty that would have matched that of her mentor Richard J. Daley and would have kept her in City Hall through the upcoming glamour of the 1992 World's Fair were smashed by the same people who put her there in the first place—Chicago's black and lakefront voters.

Harold Washington's primary victory was the result of hard work, an effective candidate, changing city demographics, and a little political luck. And in some way—political destiny. From the outset, Washington recognized that the animosity between the better organized and better financed Byrne and Daley camps left him free to woo his own natural constituency. They were ready. In short, the congressman won because, to paraphrase an old political axiom, "He saw his voters and he took 'em." Political scientists and analysts may spend years dissecting the turning points of this election, but one simple fact should not be forgotten: two white candidates evenly split more than 60 percent of the largely white vote, while the one black candidate received almost all of the black vote. Race was key in this campaign, for it would not be difficult to argue that if Harold Washington were white he would not have *entered*, let alone *won*, the 1983 Chicago Democratic mayoral primary.

X. THE PRIMARY IN PERSPECTIVE

This mayoral primary has shifted the course of Chicago politics. However, it has done so in a time-honored and traditional fashion. Once again, as in past mayoral primaries, an aspiring ethnic group has used its numbers, ingenuity, and the political system to capture the big prize. Black voters reshuffled the political deck in Chicago; the big question that remains is how many of the cardplayers will remain the same. Washington's primary win and the subsequent general mayoral victory was due in large part to the political awakening of a slumbering black community. Sounding the alarm in many black wards were the so-called "movement people,"[12] who, though they held few political offices, organized and energized the electorate. These individuals range from economic reformers to political militants, and controlling and directing their emotional appeals may be the toughest test for Washington's political skills. Like leaders of past ethnic groups who have taken power, Mayor Washington must also deal with the forces who opposed him. That task will be made considerably tougher unless the rhetoric cools and old-fashioned horse trading returns.

As for the vanquished primary contenders, their place in Chicago's political history remains uncertain. Daley is still young, more polished as a campaigner than many thought possible, and still Cook County State's Attorney. As the campaign came to a close, the son of the city's greatest political boss sounded more like a William Singer reformer than a Richard J. Daley machine politician. Yet young Daley's burden from this campaign is the belief in some ethnic communities that his challenge of Byrne led directly to Washington's election. Unfortunately for him, some Chicagoans have forgotten that as late as October 1982 he had a solid 10 percent lead over Byrne in the polls. It was his campaign strategy failures that should be criticized. His decision to have the Daleys join the Harrisons as the city's only family to have a father and son as a mayor was a sound one.

Jane Byrne's past political record and future political involvement remain debatable. She is without question a puzzling and contradictory political entity. She so wanted to immerse herself in the aura of Richard J. Daley, arguably even more than did the late mayor's own son, that she was unable to recognize what put her in office. Byrne, instinctively a crafty and streetwise politician, for reasons probably unexplainable in her own mind rejected the forces that elected her and aligned herself with the very people she had beaten—the old machine.

Byrne wanted to gobble up as many former Daleyites as possible, especially those without direct links to her mentor's son. How else can one explain her dedication to CHA director and Daley appointee Charles Swibel, a man who carried heavy political liabilities and was continuously surrounded by controversy. Demonstrating an emphasis on personal loyalty for old friends made famous by Mayor Daley, Byrne said of Swibel, "He can get the job done. . . . He knows numbers. . . . It's nice to have a lot of nice people, but you have to have somebody who can get it done."[13] These are not the words of a reform-minded woman who jolted an allegedly unbeatable political organization by appealing to the politically forgotten.

Byrne wanted to be loved and revered as Daley was, and she wanted it all now. Much of her staggering fund-raising efforts—approximately $10 million in four years—was caused in part by her desire to buy the affection she did not have time to earn. In short, Jane Byrne lost because she surrendered her own natural political senses to an overpowering desire to be a female Richard J. Daley. Political psychologists may have a field day in years to come analyzing whether she forced young Daley to grow into her major political challenger just so that she could destroy him. In other words, did she believe that eliminating the son of the departed king would leave her as the only legitimate heir to the Daley legend?

The interesting personal dramas stemming from this primary pale in comparison to the new reality of Washington's victory. Chicago politics has once again been used as a vehicle for ethnic power and as a call for political change. No one can accurately predict the final ramifications of a Washington administration, but the pride and sense of accomplishment running through black Chicago will not easily dissipate. Historically, a mayoral primary breakthrough and a City Hall takeover has been a tonic of strength for an aspiring ethnic candidate and his supporters. It will be fascinating to see whether Washington is able to close out the turbulent fourth stage of Chicago's mayoral politics by consolidating his power over the city and its Democratic party.

1. St. Clair Drake and Horace R. Cayton, *Black Metropolis: A Study of Negro Life in a Northern City* (New York: Harcourt, Brace and Company, 1945), p. 376.

2. For detailed analysis of new breed Democrats, see Paul M. Green, "Irish Chicago: The Multi-ethnic Road to Machine Success" in Melvin Holli and Peter d'A. Jones, *Ethnic Chicago* (Grand Rapids: Eerdmans, 1981).

3. Chicago *Sun-Times,* June 29, 1982.

4. Chicago *Tribune,* July 25, 1982.

5. Chicago *Sun-Times,* November 3, 1982.

6. Chicago *Tribune,* November 11, 1982.

7. Chicago *Defender,* November 13, 1982.

8. Chicago *Sun-Times,* February 18, 1983.

9. Chicago *Tribune,* February 20, 1983.

10. Chicago *Sun-Times,* February 19, 1983.

11. Washington won every precinct in wards 2, 3, 6, 16, 17, 20, 21, 24, 28, 34. Byrne's shutout ward was the 33rd while Daley's was the 23rd.

12. It is difficult to define or identify the black movement and its leadership. Loosely speaking its leadership is made up of black educators, community organizers, ministers, and involved citizens. At this time most are not elected officials but their success in 1983 has not only shaken white Chicago but it has frightened many current black politicians facing re-election in 1984 and 1986.

13. Chicago *Sun-Times,* February 9, 1983.

TABLE I

Chicago 1983 Democratic mayoral primary election results, by votes and percentages, by wards

Ward	Washington	Byrne	Daley	Winning Vote Margin	Washington Percent	Byrne Percent	Daley Percent
1	7,705	7,539	3,210	166	42%	41%	17%
2	15,882	3,244	803	12,638	80%	16%	4%
3	17,068	2,613	672	14,455	84%	13%	3%
4	17,927	3,112	1,961	14,815	78%	13%	9%
5	18,471	3,188	2,359	15,283	77%	13%	10%
6	26,979	3,075	987	23,904	87%	10%	3%
7	12,147	4,061	2,393	8,086	65%	22%	13%
8	23,946	2,426	1,325	21,520	86%	9%	5%
9	17,691	3,391	1,174	14,300	80%	15%	5%
10	6,560	15,005	6,242	8,445	24%	54%	22%
11	3,586	2,552	21,239	17,653	13%	9%	78%
12	1,750	7,633	13,510	5,877	8%	33%	59%
13	239	15,388	17,854	2,466	1%	46%	53%
14	1,669	10,403	9,912	491	8%	47%	45%
15	11,143	6,405	5,431	4,738	48%	28%	24%
16	16,604	4,061	747	12,545	77%	19%	4%
17	21,559	3,224	799	18,335	84%	13%	3%
18	11,181	7,125	12,480	1,299	36%	23%	41%
19	4,029	8,110	20,687	12,577	12%	25%	63%
20	18,313	2,883	721	15,430	84%	13%	3%
21	25,550	2,687	865	22,863	88%	9%	3%
22	1,780	3,067	3,907	840	20%	35%	45%
23	199	11,159	19,598	8,439	1%	36%	63%
24	16,296	3,598	633	12,698	79%	18%	3%
25	2,620	4,977	3,459	1,518	24%	45%	31%
26	1,488	8,208	6,610	1,598	9%	50%	41%
27	13,811	4,304	1,024	9,507	72%	23%	5%
28	15,154	2,764	727	12,390	81%	15%	4%
29	13,592	3,112	1,110	10,481	76%	18%	6%
30	516	12,571	8,520	4,050	2%	58%	40%
31	2,709	8,357	4,791	3,566	17%	53%	30%
32	2,698	7,303	8,452	1,149	15%	39%	46%
33	1,508	11,171	5,658	5,513	8%	61%	31%
34	22,601	2,676	659	19,925	87%	10%	3%
35	744	10,404	8,841	1,563	4%	52%	44%
36	343	16,486	12,940	3,546	1%	55%	44%
37	11,673	5,482	2,947	6,191	58%	27%	15%
38	385	15,180	13,275	1,905	1%	53%	46%
39	780	12,619	9,493	3,126	3%	55%	42%
40	1,005	9,417	9,226	191	5%	48%	47%
41	543	15,964	14,243	1,721	2%	52%	46%
42	6,602	9,068	8,123	945	28%	38%	34%
43	4,195	13,758	10,695	3,063	15%	48%	37%
44	4,315	12,225	8,771	3,454	17%	48%	35%
45	483	14,309	15,920	1,611	1%	47%	52%
46	5,426	8,211	6,043	2,168	27%	42%	31%
47	1,308	13,053	9,504	3,549	5%	55%	40%
48	5,024	8,160	6,385	1,775	26%	41%	33%
49	4,757	9,630	7,111	2,519	22%	45%	33%
50	1,553	12,526	10,440	2,086	6%	51%	43%
Total	424,131	387,986	344,590	36,145	36%	34%	30%
Wards Won	20	21	9				

TABLE II

Regional and Racial Breakdown of Chicago's 50 Wards

SOUTH AND WEST SIDE BLACK WARDS—19
2 - 3 - 4 - 5 - 6 - 7 - 8 - 9 - 15 - 16 - 17 - 20 - 21 - 24 - 27 - 28 - 29 - 34 - 37

SOUTHWEST SIDE ETHNIC—7
11 - 12 - 13 - 14 - 18 - 19 - 23

SOUTHEAST SIDE ETHNIC & BLACK—1
10

CENTER CITY RACIALLY MIXED & HISPANIC WARDS—5
1 - 22 - 25 - 26 - 31

NORTHSIDE LAKEFRONT INDEPENDENT WARDS—6
42 - 43 - 44 - 46 - 48 - 49

NORTH & NORTHWEST SIDE ETHNIC WARDS—12
30 - 32 - 33 - 35 - 36 - 38 - 39 - 40 - 41 - 45 - 47 - 50

III

The Resurgence of Black Voting in Chicago: 1955-1983

MICHAEL B. PRESTON

"The fact that blacks in Chicago could defeat what many considered the most powerful political machine in existence has given other black voters . . . hope."

—Michael B. Preston

One of the striking things about Chicago politics in recent years is the increasing influence of the black electorate. Black voter participation, down in the 1970s, has increased dramatically in the 1980s. The resurgence of black voting in 1982 was important to the election of a number of gubernatorial and congressional candidates in Illinois, and it was a decisive factor in the near-defeat of one of the country's most popular Republican governors, James Thompson. The most remarkable testimony to the resurgence of black voters took place in Chicago during the 1983 primary and general mayoral elections. The election of Harold Washington as mayor of the city of Chicago in 1983 can be viewed as the culmination of black dissatisfaction with the Chicago Democratic machine that had been building up for years.

The surge in black voter turnout lends support to arguments by black leaders that blacks will play an important role in the 1984 presidential election. The impact of the black electorate is likely to be felt in most local, state, and congressional elections as well. To put the current change in black political participation into perspective, however, it is necessary to take a glance at the past.

During the last twenty years, black voter turnout has been consistently a full ten percentage points lower than white voter turnout. Political scientists attribute lower turnout among blacks to lower socioeconomic status (SES) and to the history of discrimination in this country. Recently, however, blacks nationwide have been turning out in greater numbers. This is true despite their lower SES, and it looks as though political scientists will need to reconsider some of their work in this area if the upsurge continues. According to the 1980 census, blacks represent 10.8 percent of the total voting age population. This percentage translates into 17.1 million blacks of voting age in the United States, many of whom are concentrated in industrial areas of the Northern states.[1]

Figure from the 1982 nationwide elections indicate another important political development: black turnout percentages actually exceeded white turnout in eight states (California, Illinois, Indiana, Kentucky, Louisiana, Missouri, South Carolina, and Tennessee); in several other states (Michigan, Mississippi, Ohio, Oklahoma, Pennsylvania, Texas, and Virginia) the black and white turnout percentage was about equal. Nationwide, the gap in turnout between the races was the lowest it has been in twenty years (6.9%).[2]

What accounts for this resurgence? According to Eddie Williams, president of the Joint Center for Political Studies, three main factors explain the increase in black voting: 1) registration and get-out-the-vote drives targeted at blacks; 2) more black major party candidates in significant races; and 3) black opposition to President Reagan and his policies.[3] The intensity of black opposition to Reagan and his supporters was perhaps most evident in the 1982 Chicago registration and voting drive, which contributed to a 64 percent black turnout statewide among blacks, as opposed to 54.2 percent among whites.[4]

The basic argument of this chapter is that while blacks supported the Democratic machine from 1955 to 1979, their level of support never equaled their voting potential. That is to say, while their percentages were high, their numbers were low. The low black turnout over the years, especially in the primary, was a clear indication of the growing black dissatisfaction with the Democratic machine. The point here is that the Democratic organization had such little regard for black voters that it was blind to the changes taking place in the black community. Insensitivity and "tunnel vision" on the part of machine leaders led not only to the defeat of Bilandic but to that of Byrne and her candidates as well. The first section of this chapter will explore the political quiescence of black voters in Chicago from 1955 to 1979. The chapter will then proceed to demonstrate how black dissatisfaction with the Democratic machine over the years was turned into furious activity as the new decade began and how it culminated in 1983 in the election of Harold Washington.

QUIESCENCE OF BLACK VOTERS IN CHICAGO:
1955-1979

Richard J. Daley is popularly perceived as having had strong support within the black community. Black votes were "safe" votes the machine could count on. However, though Daley frequently won the mayor's office with huge margins of victory, a close examination of black voter turnout during this time clearly demonstrates that, except for the election of 1955, blacks were not major contributors to his victories. It is not that they voted against Daley; they simply did not participate. Turnout in black majority wards—wards with a black population of 50 percent or greater—was consistently lower than that of the total city by an average of 8.91 percent (see Table I). In addition, turnout in primary elections almost invariably lagged behind turnout in general municipal elections. In Chicago, due to the nature of machine politics, the primary has virtually been the "real" mayoral election. Blacks were conspicuously absent from participation in those elections.

TABLE I
Turnout in Black Majority Wards: 1955-1983

Year	Turnout for Black Wards in Mayoral Elections	Total Turnout for Whole City	Percent Difference
1955	58.35%	69%	−10.65%
1959	55.38	60.59	− 5.21
1963	64.64	73.54	− 8.9
1967	53.32	64.75	−11.43
1971	59.98	68.91	− 8.93
1975	35.37	47.3	−11.93
1977	27.25	40.05	−12.8
1979	53.15	61.03	− 7.88
1983	83.68	82	+ 1.6

In 1959, for example, the turnout in black wards for the general election was 55.38 percent, as opposed to 40.91 percent in the primary; in 1963 the black wards' general election turnout was 64.64 percent, while primary turnout was 47.51 percent. Again in 1967 the general election attracted a larger turnout percentage (53.32%) than did the primary (43.25%). Lastly, the 1971 general election turnout in black wards was substantially higher than the primary turnout: 59.8 percent versus 37.95 percent. The tendency not to exercise the right to vote in the primary nominalized any "power in numbers" blacks might have wielded. When blacks did vote, it was during the general election when their vote no longer made a difference: the machine candidate would win hands down over the Republican regardless of black voter input.

Furthermore, Daley was not necessarily interested in encouraging black organization and support. In fact, collective action by black leaders would have been viewed as disloyalty to the machine. Daley could control blacks better and prevent them from becoming a threat to him by keeping them unorganized and creating the illusion that they were dependent on him. To encourage splintering among blacks, the machine awarded patronage to individuals rather than collectively.[5] Black leaders themselves were also undermined by low turnout. Without the political clout of votes, black politicians were in a subordinate position relative to the machine. And without votes, blacks had less claim on the machine's resources. Nonetheless, the classic cyclical effect went on: blacks continued not to vote because nothing seemed to change.[6]

William Grimshaw, in his essay "Union Rule: Big City Politics in Transition," documents the gradual dissipation of black support during the latter half of Daley's tenure as mayor. He shows Daley's decreasing plurality in every ward in the city (including his own) but more drastically in the city's predominantly black wards. Grimshaw suggests that this shift was due to the racist policies inherent in the Daley administration. These policies included discriminatory practices in the areas of public security, public employment, and public housing.[7] Evidence also exists to suggest that in 1966 Daley began to de-emphasize black political mobilization and support, and that he turned to the mobilization of the white outer wards. Because Daley's core of support in white wards was so high—85 percent was not uncommon—this mobilization of the white vote was usually enough to offset losses in the black wards. Because of this shift in policies which de-emphasized black political participation, black politicians were further discouraged in their efforts to increase black voter turnout because incentives, such as patronage jobs, were reduced by this policy.[8]

Since the blacks who did vote were voting Democratic, and since the machine was receiving increasing or steady support in general municipal elections, Daley was not concerned. But someone should have been. The decreasing black turnout indicated that many blacks were potential antimachine voters. And because the black population in Chicago has been steadily increasing, the percentage of blacks who actually go to the polls takes on added meaning. They represent more actual numbers of votes as well as a bigger proportion of the city population.

Decreasing black turnout does not mean that blacks did not vote at all. What is true is that there was a substantial difference in voter participation along socioeconomic lines. Daley's machine received consistent support from non-middle-class (NMC) wards and consistently less support from middle-class wards (MC). Yet MC voters turned out more than NMC voters in presidential elections. This shows clearly that there was wasted voting potential among MC voters in municipal elections. The machine had a bigger stake in maintaining black NMC votes than MC votes. NMC voters were more numerous and consistent in their support. They were also more vulnerable to machine politicians because they needed the benefits the machine could offer.

The low voting turnout of the black middle class suggests that they may have been the strongest believers in the invincibility of the machine. For whatever reasons, the decline in voting is proportionately more acute in black middle-class wards.[9] Recent election results show that blacks in Chicago, especially middle-class blacks, have long had the potential for exercising much greater influence in local elections than they have. The MC wards rank among those giving the machine candidate the least support in local general elections. During the period from 1971 to 1977, the 8th and 21st Wards were consistently among the wards giving the machine candidate the very least support, and the 34th was in the bottom third of black wards in terms of machine support.[10]

The rankings indicate that MC voter turnout declined in relation to NMC voter turnout; yet this was only part of a larger trend of declining turnout in all black wards for mayoral general elections. Aggregate average data in Table II indicate this decline. The significance of the trend may be tested using data for the 1977 general election. Registered voters in black wards numbered 400,122 in that election. If the 1971 turnout level of 56.8 percent had persisted, 227,269 votes would have been cast in black wards in 1977. Instead, only 110,850 votes were cast. This decline of 118,220 votes represents a 106 percent decrease in black voting power.

While turnout was low or decreasing in all black wards, proportionate machine support was relatively steady in primaries and even increased in general elections. In MC wards, however, the proportionate increase was significantly larger than in NMC (7.34% larger). This observation stimulates further speculation that many

43

TABLE II

Turnout as a Percentage of Registered Voters in Black Wards: Mayoral General Elections, 1971, 1975, 1977

	1971	1975	1977	1977-1971 Difference	Aggregate Average
Middle Class Average	57.22	29.16	23.77	−33.45	36.77
Non-middle Class Average	56.68	34.69	29.26	−27.42	40.21
Difference (MC-NMC)	.54	−5.53	−5.49	6.03	−3.50
Average for All Black Wards	56.80	33.50	27.70	−29.10	39.33

blacks who were registered but stayed away from the polls did not support the machine.[11]

Presidential Elections: Evidence of an Untapped Pool

There were exceptions to the low voter turnout during Daley's reign. While black support of Daley declined, and turnout in municipal elections decreased, turnout for presidential and senatorial elections actually grew.[12] The importance of this phenomenon is the potential voting power that black voters had but did not use; the statistics on black presidential voting turnout are evidence of a pool of unused voting power.

An early indication of this was the 1964 election, in which Lyndon Johnson, an active proponent and sponsor of civil rights legislation, ran against Barry Goldwater, who openly opposed such legislation: blacks turned out in record numbers. The 1970s gave an even clearer indication of the phenomenon. The average black turnout in the 1972 and 1976 presidential elections was 67.87 percent, while it was 39.33 percent for the mayoral general elections (Chart I). Overall, if black wards had given the local mayoral candidate the same support they gave the national candidate, the latter would have received approximately ten more votes per hundred votes cast in the black wards.[13]

It should also be noted that the significance of unused voting potential varied in MC and NMC wards. In terms of percentages, the problem was more significant in MC wards, where the pool of unused votes was nearly 18 percent (Table III). In terms of numbers, however, the situation was more significant in NMC wards because more votes were cast there. Clearly, the importance of the unused pool of votes in all black wards increases as the number of black voters increases.

Low turnout among blacks during the Daley era cannot be

CHART I

Voter Turnout in Black Wards During Presidential and Mayoral Elections: 1955-1983

Source: Chicago Board of Election Commissioners and Illinois State Board of Elections

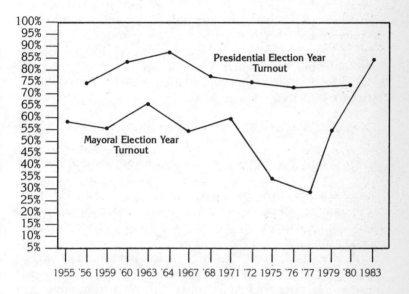

TABLE III

Percentage Gap Between Aggregate Average Democratic Support in Black Wards: Presidential and Mayoral General Elections, 1971-1977

Aggregate Average Percent Democratic Support	Middle Class	Non-middle Class
Presidential General Election	91.84	90.29
Mayoral General Election	74.10	80.19
Difference	17.74	10.10

attributed solely to Daley's political maneuvering. Several factors are relevant here, including weak ward organization, a transient population, low registration, withdrawal of the black middle class, economic poverty, and lack of a cohesive black political leadership group.

This last-named factor, the lack of leadership, deserves further discussion. Effective political leadership creates incentives for mobilization and organization, develops linkages with other groups helpful to one's own, and can use available resources to bring about the policies desired by its constituents. Ineffective leadership is dependent on external forces and cannot satisfy the needs of its constituents. This has long been the case in Chicago.[14]

From 1955 to 1979, then, blacks in Chicago lacked effective political leadership, had few other political resources, and allowed the one resource they had—the vote—to be controlled. Unorganized and alienated from both the democratic organization and the black leadership, black voters were not able to respond effectively to or defy the Democratic organization. Instead, they remained quiescent. But change was in the air.

RESURGENCE: 1979-1983

In 1979 an upswing in black voter turnout helped independent Jane Byrne oust machine candidate Michael Bilandic from the mayor's office. Blacks gave Byrne over 63 percent of their votes in the primary and even more in the general election in this major political upset.[15] In the same election three incumbent machine aldermen were defeated by black independent candidates. This was the first clear signal that the machine's strategy of relying on low but controlled turnout was vulnerable. The black middle class had returned to voting participation. In fact, black middle-class turnout in 1979 more than doubled from that of 1977. The 1979 primary also pointed more sharply to the gap between black political leaders and a majority of black voters; for every black politician had supported the regular Democratic candidate, who won only two of fourteen predominantly black wards and none of the black majority wards. It was reasonable to expect that such leaders were not likely to remain leaders very long.[16]

The ability of black voters to help defeat the machine candidate signaled to blacks the power of the vote in defeating unresponsive candidates. It also surprised the Democratic organization. The 1980 primary provided even more surprises. In 1979 Byrne received overwhelming support from the large turnout of black voters; yet just one year later, in 1980, she saw a similarly large turnout soundly defeat her choices for public office. The most telling example was the defeat of Edward Burke for state's attorney. Burke ran against Richard M. Daley, who—in an ironic twist of politics—was dubbed the "independent" candidate in this race.

There seems little doubt that a large percentage of the anti-machine vote in the 1980 primary can be attributed to Byrne's record while in office, during which time she had become part of the machine herself. Byrne's policies betrayed the trust of blacks and created a major rupture in the relationship between blacks and the machine. Particularly glaring breaches of trust for black political and community leaders during the Byrne administration were the appointment of Richard Brzeczek as police superintendent; the transit strike; school board appointments; the teachers' strike; the firefighters' strike; the CTA fare increase; and the sales tax on food and medicine. Byrne later alienated blacks even more during the summer of 1982 by replacing two blacks on the Chicago Housing Authority Board (CHA) with two pro-Byrne whites.

Almost as important as Byrne's actions was a trend over which she had no control: the growth of the black population in Chicago. Today blacks comprise roughly 40 percent of the city's population and an increasing proportion of the city's voters.

THE PRIMARY AND GENERAL ELECTIONS OF 1983

The key to Harold Washington's victory in the primary and general elections was black registration and mobilization. For example, in 1979, voter registration in Chicago stood at 1,423,476. By 1983 it had grown to 1,594,253, and the largest increase in voter registration had taken place in black wards,[17] as the following table makes clear:

TABLE IV
Changes in Voter Registration
February 22, 1979 –February 22, 1983

Location	Percent increase
17 predominately black wards	29.5%
Rest of the city	4.0%
City as a whole	11.7%

In the November 1982 election, blacks voted overwhelmingly against incumbent Republican Governor Jim Thompson. Their turnout, along with that of other white Democratic and Hispanic voters, led to one of the closest gubernatorial races in Illinois history. Thompson had been expected to win by over a million votes; instead, he won by fewer than 5,000.

Between that November 1982 election and January 1983, 62,190 more blacks were registered; an additional 30,000 plus black voters were registered between the primary in February and the general election in April. This brought the total of new black registered voters to almost 200,000. In other words, there were 615,000 to 650,000 black registered voters by the time of the 1983 primary, and by the time of the general election the number had grown to 694,000.

The Primary

The most important group in the effort to get out the vote was the Task Force, headed by Robert Starks, which consisted of 100 loosely knit organizations, P.U.S.H., and numerous black churches and students (the students were bused in from all over the state). The efforts of the Task Force were successful in the primary and even more successful in the general election.

In the primary, Harold Washington won with 37 percent of the vote, or 424,146 votes, to Mayor Byrne's 33 percent, or 388,259; Daley trailed with 30 percent, or 344,721. The significant thing about the primary is that Washington won even though he had little money, poor organization, and was opposed by eighteen of the black state legislators and nine of the black aldermen. Yet of the 482,344 blacks that voted, Washington received 80 percent or 352,100 black votes. Byrne received 89,984 black votes, and Daley received 48,379. Thus a total of 138,363 black voters voted for the two white candidates.

Harold Washington's victory in the primary shocked most political observers, including most of the newspaper writers, political analysts, and Chicago scholars—as well as the city's typical white citizen. And because Washington was black and his Republican opponent white, the general election that followed also took on a number of new dimensions. A city that had not had a Republican mayor in fifty-two years became embroiled in a racial struggle that saw many white Democrats shift to Republican Bernard Epton.

The General Election

In one of the dirtiest and most bitter campaigns in Chicago's history, Washington won by getting 51.8 percent, or 668,176 votes, to Epton's

48.2 percent, or 619,926 votes. The city turnout of 82 percent was one of the highest in Chicago's history.

The most striking thing about Washington's victory was the turnout among black voters. *No black ward turned out lower than 73 percent.* The black vote for Washington was close to 97 percent. The black middle-class wards mentioned above had the highest turnout and percent vote for Washington. For example:

6th Ward—99.3 percent Washington
8th Ward—98.6 percent Washington
21st Ward—99.2 percent Washington
34th Ward—98.6 percent Washington

And the poorest wards on the West Side, while their turnout was lower than that of the middle-class wards (74.7 percent was the lowest), gave Washington an average 96.2 percent of their vote.

The second most significant thing about Washington's victory involves another minority—the Hispanic voter. While Washington received only 12,798 Hispanic votes in the primary, he received 43,082 votes in the general election—more than 50 percent of the Hispanic vote.

CONCLUSION

The resurgence of black voting in Chicago has been building for some years now. Even before the Byrne election in 1979, black voters were becoming more independent. In the 1979 election they turned out in large numbers to vote for a mayoral candidate whom they perceived to be a reformer. And when that proved not to be the case, they defeated the mayor's candidates in 1980. In the gubernatorial election of 1982, the large outpouring of black voters gave some indication of what was likely to occur in 1983.

Indeed, the most remarkable testimony to the resurgence of black voters took place in Chicago during the 1983 primary and general election. The election of Harold Washington as mayor of the city of Chicago in 1983 may be viewed as a culmination of black dissatisfaction with the Chicago Democratic machine that had been building up for years. So dramatic was the turnout that it exceeded black voter turnout in all but one prior presidential election.

Several other things can be learned from the Washington campaign. Perhaps chief among them is that increased voter participation is especially important for black candidates. Charles Henry makes this point in his article "Racial Factors in the 1983 California Gubernatorial Campaign," in which he states that the election of black mayors has always been dependent on exceptionally high black turnout in cities with or near black majority populations (there are some exceptions to this general rule). White voters simply have not given much support to black candidates, even those slated by the Democratic party in heavily Democratic cities (e.g., Hatcher received only 14 percent of the white vote in Gary, Stokes 15 percent in Cleveland, Gibson 15 percent in Newark, Young 9 percent in Detroit, and Jackson 23 percent in Atlanta).[18] Clearly, then, black candidates have had to rely on extraordinarily large voter participation among blacks to be successful. Harold Washington's victory in Chicago was no exception. It took an extraordinary vote by blacks, with some help from Hispanics and a few whites, to put Mayor Washington into office.

Another important lesson to be drawn from this experience is that low-income voters can be stimulated into greater voter activity. The Washington campaign became a crusade, which like a raging river picked up and carried along everything in its path, including the poor and down-and-outs, who supported Washington by a large margin. The crusade also stimulated the middle class and the near poor. All of these people voted because they finally saw a chance to gain some long-needed self-respect. They also voted because they saw this campaign as Washington against the world, a position they understood only too well. In a city where many had played the game according to the rules but had not always been given the promised prizes, some had become incensed. Washington gave them new hope. Many of his supporters were voting for the first time.

It is also worth noting that white politicians did not believe that enough blacks would vote in the primary to provide Washington with a victory. They were wrong then and wrong again in the general election. Blacks may have learned a secret: voters who are predictable are never feared. Another thing that blacks may have learned is that powerlessness does not command attention; in order to demand more, one must participate more. That means not only registering, but actually voting. As Frederick Douglass once said: "Power concedes nothing without a demand; it never did and never will."

Finally, the most significant thing about the resurgence of minority voting is its impact elsewhere. Washington's victory in Chicago has been felt at the state and national level as well. The fact that blacks in Chicago could defeat what many considered the most powerful political machine in existence has given other black voters the hope that they can achieve a better society for themselves and their children. That may well be hoping for too much, but if people cannot dream or visualize a better future for themselves, they are not likely to achieve it.

---

1. Joint Center for Political Studies, *The Impact of the Black Electorate* (Washington, D.C., 1983), p. 1.

2. *Champaign-Urbana News Gazette,* April 25, 1983.

3. *Ibid.*

4. *Ibid.*

5. Michael B. Preston, "Black Politics in the Post-Daley Era," in *After Daley: Chicago Politics in Transition,* Samuel K. Gove and Louis H. Masotti, eds. (Urbana: University of Illinois Press, 1982), p. 102.

6. *Ibid.*, p. 104.

7. William Grimshaw, *Union Rule in the Schools: Big City Politics in Transformation* (Lexington, Mass.: Lexington Books, 1979), pp. 8-14.

8. Michael B. Preston, "Black Machine Politics in the Post-Daley Era," *The Chicago Politics Papers* (a series jointly sponsored by Center for Urban Affairs, Northwestern University, and The Institute of Government and Public Affairs, University of Illinois, 1979), p. 65.

9. For a more extended analysis of this problem, see Preston, "Black Politics in the Post-Daley Era," in *After Daley: Chicago Politics in Transition.*

10. *Ibid.*, pp. 94-96.

11. *Ibid.*, p. 99.

12. *Ibid.*, pp. 97-100.

13. *Ibid.*, p. 99.

14. For a more detailed discussion of the lack of political leadership, see *ibid.*, pp. 100-105.

15. *Ibid.*, p. 106.

16. *Ibid.*, p. 109.

17. Chicago Board of Election Commission, 1983.

18. Charles P. Henry, "Racial Factors in the 1984 California Gubernatorial Campaign" (paper presented at the Western Political Science Annual Meeting, Seattle, Washington, March 24, 1983), p. 7.

IV

Media Magic: Fashioning Characters for the 1983 Mayoral Race

DORIS GRABER with the assistance of Sharon O'Donnell

"How do major imbalances in campaign coverage come about? The answer is that newspeople produce them. They pick and choose whom they wish to cover and whom they wish to ignore. . . . It was a contest among 'Bad Jane,' 'Good Richie,' and 'Simon-Pure Harold' during the primary. During the general election, Harold, now a little less pure, was joined by 'Decent Bernie,' who had been largely a nonperson during the primaries. . . ."

—Doris Graber

INTRODUCTION

In the spring of 1983, Chicago had two mayoral elections instead of the usual one. Ordinarily, the Democratic winner of the primary election, with the help of an efficient Democratic machine, is assured of winning the general election; when the primary was decided, the election was decided—for all practical purposes. Things were different in 1983. In the primary, where three candidates battled for the nomination, the public awarded the prized Democratic nomination to Harold Washington by a narrow margin.

Then another major election contest began. This time it pitted the Democratic nominee, who was unpalatable to sizable numbers of Democrats and Democratic machine politicians, against a maverick Republican who had polled a mere 11,243 votes in the 1983 mayoral primary election in which over a million votes were cast. That contest has been called "Chicago's dirtiest election." It has been pictured throughout the nation and the world as a battle rife with character assassination and code words to conceal, ever so thinly, that the basic issue was the race of the candidates. Harold Washington, the Democrat and the winner by a slim 3 percent margin,

53

is black, and Bernard Epton, the Republican and near-winner, is white. Washington's Democratic predecessors in the three preceding general elections had won with landslide margins. Presumably, race, more than anything else, contributed to the closeness of the 1983 contest. Out of a total of 1,288,000 votes cast, the winner was ahead by only 48,250 votes.[1]

Since there were, in effect, two elections, we will tell the story accordingly so that the two contests can be compared. Our focus will be on one major, highly controversial element in both contests—mass media coverage. How good or bad was it compared to campaign coverage in other elections? In particular, how did the media deal with politically sensitive issues which arose because the major contenders included a woman, a black, a Jew, and a member of the well-known Chicago political dynasty.

Every Chicago election brings charges by the candidates and members of the public that the media have mishandled the campaign. The media usually counterattack by claiming that whatever is bad about the campaign is the fault of the candidates, who do not supply newspeople with desirable material for stories. The Chicago mayoral races were no exception. Charges and countercharges abounded and came from all contenders. They included threats of legal action by loser Bernard Epton, who called reporters "slime" who made him ill. He told them that his lawsuit would "make sure that any future candidate doesn't have to kiss your rear, doesn't have to bow the head."[2] That is strong language indeed. Was it deserved? How did the media cover the contests? Was it true to form, whatever that form may be? How did the performance by Chicago's news media aid or hinder the democratic process?

The Research Design

To find answers to these questions, we performed content analyses on three Chicago print media for the eight weeks leading up to the February 22nd primary and for the subsequent seven weeks leading up to the general election. Like most major American electoral campaigns, the race had gotten under way informally much earlier. By summer of 1982, pre-election polls were already recording the public's feelings about potential candidates. When they showed Mayor Jane Byrne trailing in popularity behind State's Attorney Richard M. Daley by 25 percentage points, she hired New York consultant David Sawyer to polish her image. But her official entry into the race did not come until November 23rd, 1982. Daley, son of Chicago's legendary four-term mayor, entered the fray officially on November

4th, immediately after the national elections. Congressman Harold Washington entered the race one week later, on November 10th, apparently with a good deal of reluctance. He had been a candidate in 1977 in the Democratic primary and had attracted only a small portion of the vote.

In terms of media coverage, there was relatively little election news during 1982. In fact, even the first week of January 1983 produced only few election stories. So it seemed appropriate to limit our analysis to the 1983 portions of the campaign. The papers involved in the content analysis reported here are the Chicago *Tribune* and the *Sun-Times,* which are Chicago's two major dailies, and the Chicago *Defender,* which is the largest black newspaper in the area and is published five times per week. We also analyzed *Crain's Chicago Business,* a weekly paper tailored to the needs of the business community. But that analysis will not be reported here because the number of *Crain* stories was small, and coverage features mirror those of the two major Chicago dailies.

We read and coded all campaign stories in every issue of these publications. The coding recorded which candidates were featured in the story, which of their personal qualities and professional capabilities were stressed, and how favorable or unfavorable the story was to each candidate. The coding also noted which candidate was favored by the source or sources whose comments were noted. Besides looking at candidate evaluations in the stories, we also coded every campaign issue mentioned in the story, recording whether it was described as an area of weakness or strength for a particular candidate. Finally, we coded remarks about the impact of the election on Chicago politics, predictions about the future performance of the candidates, and mentions of philosophical and ethical concerns related to the campaign. Despite the complexity of the coding decisions, reliability was high.[3]

Although financial constraints made it impossible to code television and radio news programs systematically, we randomly sampled programs on all Chicago television stations, paying particular attention to the stance of commentators and to political advertisements. We supplemented information obtained from this sample of broadcasts with information about broadcasts and advertisements published in the print media. A substantial number of news stories about the election commented about television and radio coverage and about political advertisements. The findings from the television analysis parallel the findings reported here for the newspapers in all major respects.

Coverage Objectives

Before one can appraise the merits and deficiencies of campaign coverage, one needs to set out some bench marks against which campaigns should be assessed. That is a difficult task. Perspectives vary. Performance looks different from the vantage point of the media than it does from the vantage points of the candidates. And members of the public have their distinct perspectives as well. Within all these perspectives, idealism and practicality tangle. The kinds of coverage various parties would like to see may not be feasible because it is too costly, too time-consuming, or too unattractive for mass media audiences.

In this essay we have chosen to examine media coverage from the media's perspective rather than from the perspective of candidates or of media audiences. In this triad of perspectives, the views of newspeople are most influential because they have greatest control over the substance of stories. Newspeople do not control what happens in the political arena, of course. But, protected by First Amendment guarantees, they control the spotlight of publicity. They can decide what subjects merit attention and what subjects do not, and they control the manner in which these subjects are presented. They are definitely not passive mirrors that only reflect what is put before them.

From the perspectives of journalists, campaigns are primarily "stories." To make attractive news, published stories must be interesting, with catchy headlines and exciting pictures that can hold the readers' attention from day to day. An emphasis on "hoopla and horse race"—on colorful trivia and the "who's-ahead?" and "who's behind?" and "who's attacking whom?" aspects of the race—meets that requirement. Drama, conflict, and appeals to basic human emotions are the essence of attractive news.[4]

But newspeople also view themselves as members of "the fourth branch of government," which must check whether politicians' claims and performance serve the public's interests. Therefore, careful discussion about the likely impact of a particular election on good government must be interspersed with coverage of campaign hoopla and horse race news. The serious news must be mixed with lighter fare without turning the circus atmosphere into the aura of an academic lecture hall, which would turn away a good portion of the audience. Specifically, journalists feel obligated to present information that enables voters to render verdicts about the past performance of candidates and the relationship of this performance to the office at stake in the campaign. Journalists also attempt to supply the voters with shopping lists of things the candidates intend to do. The election then becomes an endorsement of alternative shopping lists and a mandate for future performance. Finally, there is general agreement that the character of the candidates is important and that the media should shed light on it.[5]

Which of these objectives did media coverage of the 1983 mayoral elections in Chicago satisfy best? To find out, we examined 265 *Tribune* stories, 310 *Sun-Times* stories, and 169 *Defender* stories for the primaries. The numbers were larger for the general election: 341 in the *Tribune*, 380 in the *Sun-Times*, and 244 in the *Defender*. The study is therefore based on a total of 1709 print media stories. Since each story contains many different themes, the analysis proceeded on that basis. For the two elections we coded 639 and 1133 themes, respectively, in *Tribune* stories, 748 and 1288 themes in *Sun-Times* stories, and 303 and 635 themes in *Defender* stories. That makes a total of 4746 themes.

We grouped story themes into five categories. Under the heading "campaign" we included stories about the candidates' daily activities, reports about existing and future support and endorsements, and information on campaign finances. These are the topics that are frequently designated as "hoopla and horse race," with the implication that they are trivia that deserve only limited attention. A second category, called "policy," groups together themes dealing with policy issues mentioned during the campaign, such as the status of city services, affirmative action policies, and intergovernmental relations. These are the themes that, according to democratic theory, deserve most attention because they ought to be the main bases for election choices.

Topics referring to the candidates' personal attributes we placed in two categories. "Ethics" deals with themes concerning ethical behavior and philosophical positions. We examined ethics topics separately because questions like the relevance of race, gender, and religion to politics, as well as issues of fraud, deception, and corruption, were frequent targets of campaign rhetoric. "Qualities" deals with such matters as family background, mental and physical characteristics, and leadership aptitude. Democratic theorists generally consider most personal quality attributes to be legitimate factors in election choices. But they regard choices made on issue grounds to be superior. Since the election had major local and national implications for the Democratic and Republican parties, we placed themes reflecting these implications in a "party" category

COVERAGE FEATURES

Issue Coverage

As is generally true of media coverage of American elections, campaign themes turned out to be the single most widely covered subject matter. Table I presents the facts. During the primaries, 43 to 53 percent of the story themes—with the *Defender* at the high end—dealt with the comings and goings of the candidates and with their chances for winning or losing the election. In the general election, this emphasis dropped slightly. Still, 41 to 44 percent of coverage was horse race and hoopla news.

TABLE I

Distribution of Coverage Areas
(Percentage of Themes)

	PRIMARY ELECTION			GENERAL ELECTION		
	Tribune	*Sun-Times*	*Defender*	*Tribune*	*Sun-Times*	*Defender*
Campaign	43%	46%	53%	42%	41%	44%
Policy	28	24	19	20	21	23
Ethics	13	11	7	8	8	8
Qualities	11	14	19	19	19	14
Party	5	5	3	12	13	11

N (number) for Primary = *Tribune:* 639; *Sun-Times:* 748; *Defender:* 303.
N for Final Election = *Tribune:* 1133; *Sun-Times:* 1288; *Defender:* 635.

When one looks at the prominence of display of the various kinds of stories during the primaries, one finds that the media treated campaign stories less well than they did stories with other themes. As Table II shows, the average hoopla and horse race story received proportionately less prominent treatment in terms of headline size, pictorial treatment, story length, or position on a prominent page. Even though the difference is small, one may be tempted to argue that this kind of news was underplayed during the primaries and its impact reduced accordingly. But this ignores the fact that campaigning stories substantially outnumbered every other category of news. Even with lower proportions of prominent stories, they ranked at the top in actual numbers. During the general election, their proportionate rankings became more favorable in the *Tribune* and *Sun-Times* but declined in the *Defender*. Overall, Table II shows that the vast majority of election stories were not treated as exceptionally important news events, irrespective of the nature of the news themes.

In the *Tribune* and *Sun-Times,* usually 20 to 25 percent of election stories received prominent coverage; in the *Defender,* the figure averaged around 30 percent.

TABLE II

Story Prominence
(Percentage of Themes in Prominent, Average, and Minor Stories)

	PRIMARY ELECTION			GENERAL ELECTION			
	Prominent	Average	Minor	Prominent	Average	Minor	N's
Subject Matter							
			Tribune				
Campaign	20%	71%	9%	27%	68%	5%	274;472
Policy	25	69	7	18	79	4	178;228
Ethics	28	68	4	17	72	10	81;87
Qualities	22	64	14	17	80	3	73;215
Party	36	55	9	25	73	2	33;131
			Sun-Times				
Campaign	22	72	7	23	66	11	340;524
Policy	25	65	9	14	78	7	182;264
Ethics	30	69	1	22	67	11	106;97
Qualities	21	76	3	22	72	7	106;242
Party	22	70	8	19	72	9	37;161
			Defender				
Campaign	33	56	12	18	72	10	162;278
Policy	39	47	14	20	77	3	57;146
Ethics	40	45	15	37	63	—	20;49
Qualities	45	46	9	22	71	6	56;91
Party	—	87	13	20	78	3	8;71

Critics who argue that the emphasis in election news should be primarily on issues and secondarily on candidate qualifications usually decry the abundance of stories chronicling campaign events. This seems unfair when one keeps in mind that the chief objective of a campaign, after all, is the battle for votes. Thomas Patterson has observed about presidential campaigns: "Although journalists consider the campaign to have more than ritual significance, they tend not to view it primarily as a battle over the directions of national policy and leadership. It is seen mainly as a power struggle between the candidates."[6] Besides making exciting, colorful stories, hoopla and horse race news is also attractive to journalists because it constitutes "hard" facts rather than "soft" conjecture and analysis. Coverage of "hard" news protects journalists from charges that they have misunderstood the meanings of stories and misjudged their implications and ramifications. And journalists, the professional and often merciless critics of others, are surprisingly sensitive when it comes to criticism directed against them.

There are many other factors that argue against making policy issues the primary focus of media coverage. Stories dealing with policy issues lose their novelty when election campaigns stretch out over many weeks. By contrast, reports of daily activities always contain something fresh and new. Though re-examination of issues might be more beneficial, watching the passing scene of election events is far more entertaining. Moreover, most American election campaigns are not referenda on public policy issues; they could not possibly be, given the multiplicity of complex issues generally involved. Average Americans cannot comprehend them all and evaluate the positions taken by various candidates. Even when voters do understand the issues, they may still be unable to translate their positions on a variety of issues into a single vote.

Finally, and most importantly, we need to remind ourselves that better than half (just slightly less than half in *Defender* primary coverage) of the news was devoted to items other than campaign events. The impact the elections would have on the well-being of the political parties was amply discussed in all three papers. Better than one out of every five stories dealt with policy themes. These included substantial coverage of financial matters, such as taxes, the budget, fiscal management, and aid to business. There also was extensive discussion of protective services like the police and fire departments, human services like aid to the poor and to deprived groups, the civil rights of women and minorities, unemployment and job creation, as well as public education and matters of city management and city maintenance services in general.

Philosophical and ethical issues that were frequently aired included the role of power brokers in Chicago politics, the question of keeping promises and telling the truth, corruption and vote fraud, and the impact of race and sex on the campaign. In addition, there were ample references to other personal qualities of the candidates, including their trustworthiness and leadership capabilities, their ability to interact successfully with others, and their experience and prospective performance in office. Candidates' ethics and other qualities constituted better than one-fourth of all themes. These proportions held steady on a weekly basis. However, compared to the primary, there was slightly less emphasis on policy issues during the general election campaign because the candidates were seen as quite similar in their policy stands. The slack was taken up by slightly more emphasis on personal qualifications.

Balance and Bias

At first glance, then, one would have to credit the media with providing substantial coverage of public policy issues, candidate qualifications, and related political matters in addition to hoopla and horse race stories. In fact, their record of balancing campaign themes with other kinds of stories compares favorably with presidential elections, where coverage is weighted more heavily toward horse race and hoopla.

But, besides asking *what* was covered and featured, one must also ask *how* it was covered. How were policies and qualifications presented to provide a context or "frame" for evaluating the various candidacies?[7] The media pride themselves on treating candidates evenhandedly, without bias. They also strive to present enough information about the candidates so that the voters can make well-considered choices. How well did they do on these scores?

The answer to this question must be that they did not do very well. The picture that emerges is one of an imbalance of coverage. One would not expect all candidates to be covered with an equal number of positive and negative remarks: some candidates are good and deserve mostly praise, while there may be little good to say about others. The actual amount of good or bad publicity given to each candidate ought to vary accordingly. However, for the sake of balanced coverage, one would expect the media to subject all candidates to the scrutiny of friendly as well as hostile sources. While one would not look for any particular ratio of friends to enemies, one would expect a friends-enemies ratio to be similar for the major candidates. In other words, one would expect newspeople to record legitimate voices of both praise and criticism for all candidates and would not shut out either praise or criticism for a particular contender.

This expectation was not met in the Chicago election. The story is documented in Table III, which provides an overview of the known candidate preferences of individuals who raised various issues in the *Tribune, Sun-Times,* and *Defender.* The table excludes news sources whose preferences were unclear, mixed, or not mentioned. The table shows that, throughout the primary and general elections, the Jane Byrne portrait in the three newspapers, with one minor exception, was drawn far more from hostile than from friendly sources. The imbalance ran as high as three hostile sources for every one friendly source in the *Defender.* By contrast, the sources for news about the other candidates were predominantly friendly. Few anti-Daley and anti-Epton and even fewer anti-Washington sources were featured. For Richard Daley, the ratio ran as high as twelve friendly sources for every hostile one in the *Sun-Times* during the primary. As for news about Washington, it came almost entirely from friendly sources during the primaries. The contrast is particularly marked in the *Defender*, which gave only the scantiest exposure to anti-Washington sources. During the general election, the *Tribune* and *Sun-Times*—but not the *Defender*—gave somewhat increased exposure to anti-Washington sources. Still, the balance remained predominantly favorable by a wide margin.

TABLE III

Source Orientation
(Percentage of Themes)

	PRIMARY ELECTION			GENERAL ELECTION		
	Tribune	*Sun-Times*	*Defender*	*Tribune*	*Sun-Times*	*Defender*
Source Orientation						
Pro-Byrne	17%	27%	12%	9%	9%	2%
Anti-Byrne	29	26	17	11	14	7
Pro-Daley	23	24	10	1	1	—
Anti-Daley	8	2	6	—	—	1
Pro-Washington	20	21	52	34	38	74
Anti-Washington	2	1	3	19	11	2
Pro-Epton	1	1	—	18	20	5
Anti-Epton	—	—	1	8	8	10
N's	(639)	(748)	(303)	(714)	(828)	(508)

Much of the negative publicity given to Jane Byrne concerned the record of her administration. Her achievements were measured by the yardstick of her campaign promises and, not unexpectedly, found wanting. Balanced treatment would have required subjecting her rivals to comparable scrutiny. The fact that the challengers had not served as mayor did not preclude examination of their records and their promises in other public offices. The major Democratic challengers, as well as the Republican primary election nominee, had all been state legislators. Harold Washington was an incumbent U.S. congressman, and Richard Daley held the office of state's attorney. Yet the challengers were largely spared having these records examined and possibly tarnished. Moreover, their promises of future performance received little intensive scrutiny. Newspeople might have assessed the feasibility of their promises and the likelihood that the candidates would try to implement them.

Table IV traces the consequences of this choice of sources when policy issues, ethics questions, or the candidates' personal qualifications were under consideration. In each case the table presents the percentage of negative themes in that subject area. The percentage was computed from the sum of negative and positive comments made by enemies as well as friends of the candidates. Neutral and mixed comments were omitted from the calculations; but their number is indicated (in the table under the heading "Excluded Themes") to show the steady rise in neutral commentary as the election progressed.

The table shows that even when news from favorable sources mutes the impact of unfavorable sources, Jane Byrne's image was by far the worst and Harold Washington's image by far the best. There were substantial differences as well as similarities among the three papers. In each case, comments about the ethics of the candidates' behavior were the most negative. With some exceptions, personal qualities received less negative commentary than did policy stands. Except for the *Defender,* which treated Richard Daley most negatively, Jane Byrne headed the villain list. With minor exceptions, Washington received the most favorable treatment in all three papers throughout the entire campaign, even though the *Tribune* and *Sun-Times* had endorsed Daley during the primary. Of the three papers, the *Tribune* recorded the most negative comments about Washington, while the *Defender* was most positive toward him, largely because of its concentration on him as its favored and highly praised candidate. While the rate of negative themes about Washington picked up sharply after the primaries, the impact was lessened because, in contrast to the primaries, neutral themes increased sharply and dominated in the discussion of policy issues during the general election coverage.

Spotlighting Candidate Characteristics

Personal qualifications constituted an average of 25 percent of total coverage in the print media, when one adds questions of ethics to other personal qualities. This was one area in which television coverage differed somewhat from newspaper coverage: television stories put heavier emphasis on personality attributes at the expense of an emphasis on policy issues. However, the print figures on coverage of personal qualifications are somewhat understated because much of the information about policy issues and about the campaign also

TABLE IV

Selected Negative Story Themes

(Positive Themes Included in Calculations; Mixed and Neutral Themes Excluded)
(*Dashes indicate absence of positive as well as negative themes)

	PRIMARY ELECTION			GENERAL ELECTION		
	Policy Issues			**Policy Issues**		
Candidate	Tribune	Sun-Times	Defender	Tribune	Sun-Times	Defender
Byrne	70%	68%	63%	95%	76%	43%
Daley	57	24	67	85	50	71
Washington	20	10	0	64	35	19
Epton	—*	25	—	71	52	78
N's	(119)	(141)	(38)	(78)	(93)	(39)
Excluded Themes:	(50)	(36)	(15)	(99)	(115)	(65)
	Ethical Conduct			**Ethical Conduct**		
Byrne	92	86	83	100	92	100
Daley	86	64	—	75	100	100
Washington	71	67	—	75	88	75
Epton	—	—	—	75	11	100
N's	(56)	(59)	(12)	(26)	(35)	(16)
Excluded Themes:	(18)	(15)	(5)	(21)	(18)	(13)
	Personal Qualities			**Personal Qualities**		
Byrne	44	33	33	61	81	50
Daley	29	26	—	67	50	50
Washington	0	14	10	54	64	12
Epton	0	—	50	54	64	73
N's	(56)	(86)	(44)	(134)	(146)	(56)
Excluded Themes:	(16)	(17)	(12)	(56)	(67)	(26)

conveyed information about the personal qualities and qualifications of the candidates.

Since it is important for voters to compare the contenders in a race, we examined the data presented in Table V to check out similarities and differences in treatment of the various candidates. Did they receive similar amounts of publicity, and were they covered fairly evenly—along the same dimensions? Here again, the answer is no. Coverage, obviously, was *not* equal on either score. Most strikingly, Bernard Epton, the Republican contender, received barely any coverage at all during the primary. He was indeed "the invisible man," as he so bitterly complained. Although most political observers granted that all three Democratic hopefuls had a chance to win the primary, the alternatives represented by a Washington-Epton, Daley-Epton, and Byrne-Epton contest were hardly weighed in the media. If voter enlightenment was a goal, they certainly should have been.

Had the three papers treated all candidates roughly equally, the percentage of coverage listed for each kind of theme should have ranged between 20 and 30 percent in the primaries. During the general election, the percentages allotted to Washington and Epton should have been similar. Obviously, this was not the case. During the primary, the *Tribune* and *Sun-Times* gave a disproportionate amount of coverage to Jane Byrne, while the *Defender* dwelt largely on Washington. Byrne's policies and the ethics of her conduct received particularly heavy attention in the *Tribune*. The *Tribune* also focused heavily on Daley's personal qualifications but slighted questions about the ethics of his campaign.

That such choices were idiosyncratic to each paper becomes clear when one compares coverage among the three papers. In the *Sun-Times* and *Defender,* for instance, there was a much better discussion balance between the policy stands of Byrne and Daley than was true in the *Tribune*. Similarly, neither the *Sun-Times* nor the *Defender* dwelt disproportionately on Daley's personal qualifications. Nor were ethical concerns in the Daley campaign de-emphasized in these two papers. In fact, the *Defender,* unlike the other two papers, put the spotlight on ethics issues in the Daley campaign.

The conclusions to be drawn from comparing coverage is that there was ample story material so that the media could have supplied the voters with balanced accounts in which comparable dimensions were sketched out for each candidate. A voter, eager to compare the policy positions or integrity of the candidates, for instance, would then have been able to find adequate information for all three on these scores. By and large, 1983 primary election news did not meet this need.

The situation was similar during the general election campaign. Then all three papers devoted the lion's share of coverage to Washington. Epton received a mere 16 percent of exposure in the *Defender,* compared to 84 percent for Washington; in the *Tribune,* it was 30 percent for Epton, compared to 70 percent for Washington; the *Sun-Times* showed the best balance: it finished with 39 percent for Epton compared to 61 percent for Washington. However, when one looks at the distribution of coverage among various kinds of themes, the *Sun-Times* actually turns out to be less well-balanced than the other papers. For instance, it devoted 24 percent of Wash-

TABLE V

Coverage for Each Candidate
(Percentage of Themes)

Candidates	Byrne	Daley	Washington	Epton	Other Democrats N's

TRIBUNE – PRIMARY ELECTION

Candidates	Byrne	Daley	Washington	Epton	Other Democrats N's
Campaign	20%	26%	24%	2%	28% (251)
Policy	41	16	16	—	27 (153)
Ethics	42	9	21	—	28 (76)
Qualities	15	39	17	3	26 (66)
Party	26	17	22	13	22 (23)

TRIBUNE – GENERAL ELECTION

	Byrne	Daley	Washington	Epton	Other Democrats N's
Campaign	28	2	36	21	14 (222)
Policy	10	3	55	29	4 (119)
Ethics	22	—	54	11	13 (46)
Qualities	20	—	53	21	6 (19)
Party	23	—	66	11	— (70)
Primary N's	(161)	(127)	(116)	(11)	(154)
Final N's	(121)	(7)	(270)	(116)	(47)

SUN-TIMES – PRIMARY ELECTION

	Byrne	Daley	Washington	Epton	Other Democrats N's
Campaign	38	18	20	3	21 (313)
Policy	35	26	15	2	23 (170)
Ethics	53	14	10	1	22 (73)
Qualities	24	23	23	1	30 (102)
Party	20	30	27	13	10 (30)

SUN-TIMES – GENERAL ELECTION

	Byrne	Daley	Washington	Epton	Other Democrats N's
Campaign	25	2	36	25	12 (279)
Policy	14	1	57	26	2 (121)
Ethics	30	—	34	28	8 (50)
Qualities	21	—	44	31	4 (132)
Party	14	—	54	29	2 (90)
Primary N's	(247)	(141)	(126)	(18)	(156)
Final N's	(143)	(7)	(292)	(184)	(46)

DEFENDER – PRIMARY ELECTION

	Byrne	Daley	Washington	Epton	Other Democrats N's
Campaign	24	14	55	—	7 (149)
Policy	39	27	31	—	4 (52)
Ethics	21	32	32	—	16 (19)
Qualities	10	12	69	—	10 (52)
Party	50	—	50	—	— (4)

DEFENDER – GENERAL ELECTION

	Byrne	Daley	Washington	Epton	Other Democrats N's
Campaign	8	1	69	11	10 (163)
Policy	1	—	80	13	6 (96)
Ethics	4	—	44	22	30 (23)
Qualities	2	—	73	20	6 (66)
Party	10	—	78	10	2 (41)
Primary N's	(66)	(47)	(142)	(0)	(21)
Final N's	(20)	(2)	(280)	(52)	(35)

ington commentary to policy themes, compared to 17 percent for Epton. In the *Tribune,* Epton was ahead in coverage of policy themes with a score of 29 to 24 percent. There was a similar five percentage point spread in the *Defender,* but it went in the opposite direction: policy themes constituted 28 percent of the coverage for Washington but only 23 percent for Epton. Similar imbalances marked the other coverage areas, with papers differing in their choice of either Washington or Epton as the candidate deserving proportionately more attention for particular themes. Again, the obvious message is that choices made by journalists, rather than the nature of available news, made the difference. If journalists had desired more balanced coverage, they could have attained it.

The effects of unbalanced coverage were diluted somewhat by media coverage of the candidate debates. The debates, which were watched off and on by more than six million viewers, permitted the public to see the contenders side by side, responding to the same questions. This made it easy to compare how the candidates conducted themselves in tension-filled situations. Viewers also could assess the general quality of the answers and could discern major differences in policy stands.

The debates also served to erase some of the advantages that more affluent candidates gained by being able to get more exposure for their commercials. Harold Washington was the chief beneficiary on that score. By February 2nd, when the debates were over, he had not been able to air any television commercials. The debates lent legitimacy to his candidacy by giving him citywide exposure and by showing off his considerable oratorical and political talents.

The Reasons for Unbalanced Coverage

How do major imbalances in campaign coverage come about? The answer is that newspeople produce them. They pick and choose whom they wish to cover and whom they wish to ignore. They also select the individuals whose views they will report. If they inadvertently—or for reasons of convenience or by design—draw from a particular pool of sources, the news will reflect this because it is filtered through the particular perspectives of the individuals selected as news sources. One might argue that imbalances in the views of news sources and in the attention paid to various candidates reflected the realities of the 1983 Chicago mayoral election—that the media merely mirrored reality. It was a contest among "Bad Jane," "Good Richie," and "Simon-Pure Harold" during the primary. During the general election, Harold, now a little less pure, was joined by "Decent Bernie," who had been largely a nonperson during the primaries because Republicans usually make a poor showing in Chicago mayoral campaigns.

Obviously, the situation was not that clear-cut. As it turned out, Republican Epton almost became Chicago's mayor, a contingency that could and should have been foreseen by the media once the slate of candidates was known. But established coverage patterns die hard, especially when they are reinforced by pack journalism. Since it is customary for Chicago's media to view Republican candidacies as doomed, they treated 1983 as no exception. In the tradition of follow-the-leader pack journalism, few reporters strayed from the fold.

Similarly, there was no reason to make saints or near-saints out of any of the contenders. All of them were flawed to some degree and had prominent detractors who were eager to discuss these flaws. Harold Washington's many enemies, for instance, would have loved an opportunity to discuss his repeated failures to pay various kinds of taxes and fees and his brief jail term for nonpayment. But the media avoided much, though not all, of this kind of coverage by presenting Washington almost exclusively through the eyes of friendly sources.

In the absence of hard data, one can only guess at the reasons for tilting coverage in favor of the challengers and against the incumbent. There seems to be a trend in recent elections to attack incumbents in order to strip them of the advantages of incumbency while sparing the challengers from comparably harsh treatment.[8] Attacks are easy because the incumbent has a performance record for the specific job at stake in the election. Since most political decisions are controversial, it is easy to find people who are prepared to orchestrate the theme of "throw the rascals out." Discussions with newspeople involved in the Chicago campaign also point to their generally anti-Byrne orientations as another reason. She had antagonized newspeople on many occasions by her policies as well as by her squabbles with reporters. There were also charges that Jane Byrne's sex was a factor—that women in politics are allegedly fair game for exceptionally harsh criticism. However, most media people deny that. We will have more to say about that later.

Unwillingness to criticize a black contender at the risk of being labeled "racist" was another factor that was freely acknowledged by media people as well as by Byrne and Daley media consultants.

David Sawyer, who worked for Jane Byrne, expressed typical concerns when he said: "So the thing we feared most was the race issue. That's why we couldn't attack Washington: she was already seen as unfair to blacks, and whites, simply perceiving her as unfair, would switch their support to Daley."[9]

With Byrne and Daley avoiding attacks on Washington, and newspeople not eager to search out other Washington foes or to dwell on his flaws on their own in news commentary, Washington's record remained largely unsullied. Jane Byrne, the incumbent mayor, was the target of negative criticism by the Washington and Daley campaigns as well as by news commentators. Fired on from three camps, she was bound to be most heavily bloodied. Daley received a moderate amount of criticism, largely from the Washington camp. Byrne and Daley's restraint in criticizing Washington spared them largely, though not entirely, from the racist label. Bernard Epton did not fare as well. Despite his liberal antiracist, pro-civil rights record, and his repeated disavowals of racist motives, most of his attacks on Washington during the final campaign were tagged as "racist."

Medialities in the Campaign

In the evaluation of media performance during a campaign, it is not sufficient to look at the frequency with which certain subjects are covered, the distribution of that coverage among various candidates, and the negative and positive thrusts of coverage. One must also look for certain key factors in coverage which, irrespective of frequency, have a profound impact on the campaign. Political scientist Michael Robinson calls such factors "medialities." He defines them as "events, developments, or situations to which the media have given importance by emphasizing, expanding, or featuring them in such a way that their real significance has been modified, distorted, or obscured."[10]

There was only one major mediality in the 1983 mayoral contest: the question of racism. By comparison, everything else paled. There were three other emotion-tinged issues that could have been exploited. One was that Jane Byrne is a woman and that some of her failings had been attributed in the past to her sex. Similarly, the media could have played the dynasty issue heavily with constant comparisons between Richie Daley and his famous father. The fact that Bernard Epton would have been the city's first Jewish mayor could also have been a major focus for media discussion. All these factors were mentioned, of course.

The woman's issue received greatest attention in the wake of a feature article in the *Sun-Times,* which characterized Jane Byrne as a disappointed, indecisive female whose job performance was marred by the deficiencies characteristic of her sex. There is no question that the media stereotyped Jane Byrne. It was Bad Jane who had broken her promises, exaggerated her achievements, run up huge debts, kept bad political company, and exhibited a mercurial temper. When she appeared to behave differently during the campaign, the press attributed this to her campaign consultant who had created a "New, Steadfast Jane."

But there was rarely any hint of stereotyping Jane Byrne as the prototypical woman candidate. The glaring exception was the so-called psycho-biography in the *Sun-Times* that analyzed Byrne in almost Freudian terms.[11] By and large, however, the critique of Jane Byrne was not antifeminist. She was called "Lady" Jane at times, or the "restless, fierce-eyed Queen," or "Attila, the Hen," but it never was routinely the "lady mayor" or the "woman mayor." Unlike commentary early in her administration, there were no references to raging hormones or female proclivities for snap decisions and flip-flops. It may well be that her proof that a woman could handle the mayor's job had reduced criticism expressed in antifeminist terms. Many of the things that the stereotyped female executive cannot do, such as getting competent men to take orders from her or showing strength and leadership, could not be charged against her anymore.

Some people feel that the fact that Jane Byrne is a woman contributed to the harshness of criticism. "They would never do that to a man," was a common remark. Maybe so, but the fact remains that harsh criticism of incumbents of both sexes has become a steady feature of election coverage.[12] Jane Byrne was treated far worse than her opponents were; but, with minor exceptions, what was said about her did not specifically reflect on the political and administrative capabilities of women as a group.

The media also refrained, by and large, from stereotyping Richard Daley as merely an offshoot of the mighty Daley dynasty. Although Daley himself frequently traded on the name of his father during speeches and in television commercials, media stories did not dwell heavily on comparisons between father and son. Some remarks were made about shared problems in making speeches, to be sure; the fact that Daley was taking elocution lessons to correct his "dese," "dems," and "doses" and frequent slips in syntax was the subject of some tongue-in-cheek commentary. One writer, comparing father and son, called the senior Daley "a symbol of mastery of the urban jungle" who made Chicago "the city that worked." By contrast, this writer characterized his son as "a born-again preppie with Oxford-cloth, button-down shirts . . . whose mother's presence with him in public is a reminder that he is still 'The Son,' not quite a man in his own right."[13] The *Tribune's* editorial endorsement of Daley also called his family's political traditions an important factor. "If young Richard just lives up to that part of the tradition, he's the best bet for this city in the primary."[14] But on the whole, the press treated the Daley name as merely an asset in name recognition and little more.

Even less was made of the fact that Bernard Epton, the Republican challenger, who was pictured as a somewhat eccentric, irascible loner, is Jewish. There were some references to the fact that Jewish voters, particularly in the liberal wards along the lakefront, might be torn between ethnic pride and their desire to foster the election of a black leader in line with pro-civil rights attitudes. The media also quoted crowds yelling "Jew Boy" at Epton while urging him to defeat Washington. But Epton never became "the" Jewish candidate. He merely happened to be a candidate who was Jewish and might become the city's first mayor of that faith.

The approach was quite different for Harold Washington. From the start, he was *the* black candidate. Hardly a story failed to refer in some way or other to the fact that Harold Washington was black and that his primary base of support came from members of his race; the phrase "the black candidate" became almost a part of his name. After his victory in the primary, television interviewers kept asking people how they felt about the possibility of a black as the next mayor. When answers skirted the race issue, reporters kept pressing for racial statements. Newspapers and television stations started a series of special features describing how other major cities had fared under the administration of black chief executives. Even aldermen whose race had not been made explicit in prior news stories began to be referred to by their race.

It would be unfair to make the media bear the primary responsibility for casting the discussion of Washington's candidacy into a black-versus-white perspective. The candidates and their associates did make racism a major theme. For example, Harold Washington accused Bernard Epton of running "one of the most racist campaigns" in recent American history.[15] And he began his campaign by telling a black audience that "it's our turn" and claiming that "every group, when it reaches a certain population percentage, automatically takes over. They don't apologize . . . they just move in and take over."[16] Many whites bridled when these remarks were featured in the news and called them black racism. Blacks countered by saying that these were expressions of ethnic pride which were not intended to exclude whites from power on racial grounds.

During the last week of the primary, racism charges escalated when Daley and Washington both claimed that Byrne was using the issue to win votes. The media reported distribution of literature that claimed that a vote for Daley, instead of Byrne, was likely to sweep Harold Washington into office. Indeed, Edward Vrdolyak, the Cook County Democratic Party Chairman and 10th Ward alderman, in the same vein, was quoted as telling his followers at a political rally that "a vote for Daley is a vote for Washington. . . . It's a racial thing. Don't kid yourselves."[17] The controversy over whether reports about this remark lost the primary election for Jane Byrne will never be settled. It is clear from the record, though, that charges of racism were influential factors in the election.

Still, while racial remarks by partisans abounded, the media's reporting strategies exaggerated the situation. They eagerly picked up inflammatory comments and kept them alive by frequent repetition. In fact, the media projected a racially focused campaign from the moment Washington entered the contest. As early as November 29th, the *Tribune* ran a feature editorial by Leanita McClain entitled "The Racial Truth of Politics," which asked Chicagoans to "acknowledge that race is going to be an issue whether anyone wants it to be or not." She urged Chicagoans: "Don't try to sweep it aside, deal with it."[18]

What is more, newspeople, though they bemoaned the injection of the racism issue into the campaign, went out of their way to turn trivia into news. They picked up a lot of inconsequential racial references and blew them out of proportion. In the process, they increased the importance of the racism issue in the campaign for voters and for onlookers. They also gave Chicago a worldwide reputation for far greater interracial hostility than the facts warranted.[19]

For example, late in January, Jane Byrne, while addressing an audience of De Paul University students, was naming black members of her administration in response to a question about appointments of black officials. She commented about Lenora Cartwright, her commissioner of human services, that she "has her master's degree in social work, excellent. She happens to be black, but she's good."[20] Byrne then made a similar comment about Elmer Beard, Jr., executive director of the Chicago Housing Authority.

One story graphically illustrates the magnification and misuse of racial angles and racist charges. The story has become familiar to millions of people because it flashed not only around Chicago but around the nation and the world, as an international corps of news reporters surveyed and reported on the Chicago scene.[21] It happened during the general election campaign.

On Palm Sunday, Harold Washington, accompanied by former Vice President Walter Mondale, went to worship at St. Pascal's Church on Chicago's Northwest Side. Candidates Washington and Epton both had been invited earlier for a political meeting at the church, but those arrangements had fallen through because of scheduling difficulties. So Washington had decided to join the congregation in prayer instead. The agreement with the church leadership had been that this would not be a political rally, and newspeople would not be welcome inside the church to cover the event. Moreover, Washington and his party were to arrive at the church at the beginning of services, just like other worshippers.

It did not turn out that way. Washington and Mondale arrived at the church toward the end of the service with a bevy of newspeople in tow. In front of the church, Washington and Mondale were booed and jeered by a crowd of 150 people who had gathered outside; of these, 20 to 25 were members of the church, but the rest were strangers. Many of the protesters wore Epton buttons and shouted his name. There were no racial epithets. The epithets recorded were "crook," "tax cheater," "baby-killers" (referring to the visitors' stand on abortion), and "carpetbagger" (referring to Mondale). The whole incident differed little from booing episodes involving Jane Byrne, Richard Daley, and Bernard Epton on other occasions.

Inside the church, 800 to 900 parishioners were finishing their prayers. Washington and Mondale, who entered the church by a side door, decided to leave since they had come too late for the service; they were not forced out of the church. Nonetheless, the incident made the front pages of all the papers and was billed as a racial insult. Washington's campaign managers even incorporated it into one of their television advertisements, putting it on a par with Hitler's persecution of the Jews and the assassinations of John F.

Kennedy and Martin Luther King. The media treatment of this incident at St. Pascal's church is a perfect example of a mediality.

What evidence is there that racism was less important in the campaign than media coverage suggested? There is some, but it will never convince those who believe that all white people are inherently racist and reject black candidates for that reason. In the words of a *Defender* editorial: "In this city where segregation is a baptismal font in which nearly all whites dip their fingers, a mayoral contest in which a Black candidate is opposed by a white candidate—there is no way to keep race out of the contest." Then it accused Bernard Epton of racism, alleging that his supporters gathered around him solely because they objected to his opponent's race.[22]

Many white voters openly rejected this notion of inherited guilt. For instance, the media reported numerous complaints by white readers who gave reasons other than race for finding Harold Washington unacceptable. They felt that it was unfair and presumptuous to attribute motivations to them which they had never expressed. As one woman put it bluntly: "I am not voting for Epton because he is white. I am voting for Epton because Harold Washington's record stinks. If Washington did not have the kind of record he has or if there was a candidate who happened to be black who was a good candidate, I'd vote for him. I'm no racist, and I resent the way that word is hurled at whites who are voting for Epton."[23] One may choose to believe her, and the thousands like her, rather than those who charge that she, and other whites, are merely concealing their conscious or unconscious racist motivations.

Similarly, a *Sun-Times* poll, asking people for reasons why they preferred various candidates over their opponents found that the ability of the candidate to provide services used by the voter was the chief criterion. Most voters indicated that their choice was based on strong preferences for a particular candidate rather than on the desire to defeat one of the other contenders. The race of the candidate was mentioned as a vote attraction by a sizable number of respondents only in the case of Harold Washington. Twelve percent of his supporters claimed that they would vote for him "because he's black."[24] In an exit poll, conducted after the primary, two out of three white voters said that Washington's race was not important in their vote. Most Washington opponents claimed that they rejected him because they were concerned about his income tax conviction.[25] In an exit poll after the general election, only 4 percent of the blacks polled and 5 percent of the whites gave race as the reason for their choice. A majority of Epton voters claimed to vote for him because they perceived him as more honest, while a majority of the Washington voters saw him as a better leader.[26] One may choose to believe that, in most instances, these were their primary motivations.

A check of individuals and organizations endorsing Washington's candidacy reveals large numbers of Chicago whites who openly declared their support for him and whose endorsements apparently were based on concerns other than race. For instance, Washington was endorsed by most of Chicago's white labor unions, who liked his record on labor issues. He also received support from many white churches and their congregations, who believed that he could unify the city, and from many liberal Democrats, who agreed with his political philosophy.

Finally, when election day rolled around, Harold Washington won only because his support in the black community was supplemented by support from 18 percent of the city's white voters. These votes came from all parts of the city and were not limited to the wine-and-cheese set along the city's northern lakefront.[27] Washington also received much of his financial support from whites in Chicago, Chicago's suburbs, and across the nation, demonstrating that large numbers of whites do support black candidates.

It is true that, contrary to the usual patterns in Chicago's mayoral elections, many Democrats crossed party lines and voted for a Republican. But even that was not so extraordinary under the circumstances presented by the election that it could be explained only as a vote against Washington's race. First of all, Washington was a flawed candidate. Bernard Epton, the alternative choice, despite his questionable style of campaigning, had a good personal and public service record. Moreover, Washington's candidacy was very threatening to many Chicagoans because he had vowed to dismantle the Democratic machine and end political patronage. By contrast, Epton reassured the beneficiaries of machine politics that he could live with the machine and with the patronage system.

Secondly, crossing party lines has not been unusual in Chicago in the past. After all, large numbers of Chicago Democrats have voted for Republican presidents, governors, and state's attorneys. There also is precedent for voting against the Democratic machine's choice. It happened in the two most recent primary elections, when the voters endorsed Jane Byrne in 1979 and Harold Washington in 1983 against the recommendations of the Democratic machine.

All this adds up to solid evidence that many factors besides race do play a part in people's voting choices, even in Chicago. The media could have chosen to make religion a pivotal factor in the campaign. They did not. They could have played the gender issue heavily, but they did not. Nor did they emphasize the dynasty factors. By contrast, they overplayed race and in the process made it more significant than it need have been. It is difficult to judge how much harm this approach did to racial harmony in the city and to the reputation of Chicago and its citizens around the nation and the world.

INTERRACIAL MAYORAL CAMPAIGNS IN PERSPECTIVE

To check whether media emphasis on the racism issue was peculiar to the 1983 Chicago contest, we scanned the coverage of fifteen other recent big-city mayoral election contests in which black candidates were involved. These were the four campaigns of Tom Bradley in Los Angeles in 1969, 1973, 1977, and 1981; the three campaigns of Kenneth A. Gibson in Newark in 1970, 1974, and 1978; the three campaigns in Atlanta which elected Maynard Jackson in 1973 and 1977 and Andrew Young in 1981; Coleman Young's three campaigns in Detroit in 1973, 1977, and 1981; and the primary campaigns of Harold Washington in Chicago in 1977 and W. Wilson Goode in Philadelphia in 1983.

We checked the coverage of these races in *The New York Times* because this provided a single standard for comparison, drawn from a paper that is a pace-setter for print and electronic media throughout the United States and the world. Examining *New York Times* coverage has another advantage. An out-of-town paper extracts the most salient, most interest-arousing features of a race for its limited amount of coverage of an out-of-town election. The local press normally features a much larger number of issues, and thus key issues stand out less clearly in frequency counts. This is why comparisons of coverage by *The New York Times* with coverage by the three Chicago newspapers, the *Los Angeles Times,* and the *Detroit News* generally showed that key issues are easiest to detect in *The New York Times*.

If one calls it heavy emphasis on race issues when 50 percent or more of all election stories dwell on racial motivations, then roughly half of the contests we examined were given heavy emphasis, similar to the Chicago situation in 1983. The patterns of coverage are illuminating. The race issue generally received heavy emphasis in the black candidate's first election. During the second election patterns varied, with emphasis either increasing, decreasing, or remaining stable. Beyond that, emphasis on racial issues dropped sharply. Apparently, once all the dire forecasts about racial problems and tensions had given way to the more pleasant realities of actual performance by black mayors, racial issues assumed a much diminished role.

Specifically, for Tom Bradley and Kenneth Gibson, emphasis on racial issues was high for the first election, increased for the second, but dropped for the third and, in Bradley's case, the fourth as well. In Maynard Jackson's case, emphasis on race was high for the first contest, dropped considerably to a 60 percent range for the second contest, and remained there when Andrew Young succeeded Jackson in 1981. For Coleman Young, 44 percent of the stories during his 1973 and 1977 campaigns emphasized race issues, followed by a sharp drop during his 1981 campaign.

Let us turn to the two primary contests. Harold Washington's chances of winning the 1977 Democratic primary in Chicago were deemed slim; accordingly, he received little coverage of any kind, and questions of racial problems remained subdued. In the 1983 Philadelphia primary in which Wilson Goode was a candidate, it was the general consensus among newspeople that race was not a major factor. It therefore received only moderate attention in *New York Times* stories. Still, headlines pointed to it as if it were a newsworthy surprise that racism was absent. For example, on April 12th, 1983, the paper headlined the fact that "Race is a Muted Issue in Philadelphia." A May 12th headline made an invidious comparison of Philadelphia's primary with Chicago's: "It's not Chicago, Philadelphia Democrats Say of Their Primary."

The comparisons with other interracial mayoralty contests thus indicate that media coverage of the Chicago contest reflects common patterns, especially for major cities faced for the first time with the prospects of a black candidate defeating a white challenger for the mayor's office. This makes the lessons drawn from the Chicago situation all the more urgent.

THE IMPACT OF COVERAGE ON ELECTION OUTCOME

What effect did media images have on the thinking of Chicago voters? The answers are mixed. In line with media coverage, *Sun-Times* polls showed a steady increase in the number of voters who believed that whites would not vote for blacks.[28] On the other hand, many voters did not buy the media's picture of the incompetence of Jane Byrne. There are several reasons for this. For one, the major areas of concern in city politics are areas where citizens have direct experiences. They are therefore likely to stick with their own observations rather than with media analyses. The polls bear this out when they show a direct relationship between voter appraisals and the adequacy of city services in different parts of the city. Secondly, media stories were partly counterbalanced by the advertising campaigns of the major candidates, which were designed to counteract adverse media images. We also know from public opinion polls that the most widely used criterion for judging Richard Daley was his family connection, despite the media's soft-pedalling of the issue.[29] Voters expressed like or dislike for Daley in terms of their appraisal of his famous father: good or bad, they thought it would be "like father, like son." Again, people's own impressions were dominant, and those impressions were in tune with images created by Daley's campaign commercials.

When it came to judging Washington and Epton, most voters had little personal knowledge with which to make a choice. When that happens, the media are far more likely to make an impact. As discussed earlier, Washington's media image was highly favorable compared to Byrne's and Daley's. Compared to Epton, Washington had the vast advantage of becoming a household word for voters long before Epton was thrust on the scene. That advantage grew during the general election campaign when Washington received the lion's share of media attention. Though Epton's image during the general election campaign was, on balance, positive, it was never as positive as the image established for Washington during the primaries and continued during the final campaign. Many voters' impressions of the candidates reflected these images.

Of course, it would be wrong to claim that Washington made a good impression on many voters only because the media fashioned his image that way. There are candidates who have an excellent media presence, and Washington is one of them. There are others who lack this quality, and Epton is a graphic example. But the media enhanced what was there. Just as a cartoonist picks out major features and exaggerates them to the point of distortion, so the media caricatured both Washington and Epton. It enhanced Washington's image and detracted from Epton's picture, and this left its mark on voters' minds.

In the end, the candidate with the most favorable media image won, against great odds in the primary as well as in the general election. In a close election, like the 1983 race, it is difficult to tell

Mayor Jane Byrne made national headlines when she temporarily moved into the city's toughest housing project, Cabrini-Green. Here she campaigns among her erstwhile neighbors showing her political as well as athletic abilities. *(Chicago* Sun-Times)

Reprinted by permission: Mike Peters, editorial cartoonist, Dayton Daily News.

The media's reporting strategies exaggerated inflammatory comments and in fact projected a racially focused campaign from the moment Washington entered the race.

In late January as the three-way Democratic mayoral campaign became emotionally charged, State's Attorney Richard M. Daley and U.S. Congressman Harold Washington attempted to defuse racial feelings in a joint rally held at the First Lutheran Church, located on Daley's home turf in the Bridgeport neighborhood. *(Chicago* Sun-Times)

Baby kissing is a time honored political ritual, and here candidate Epton is seen bestowing an affectionate hug on the offspring of a potential Republican voter.   *(Lee Balterman)*

Candidate Bernard E. Epton became a popular choice of many Chicago police officers after Harold Washington made a campaign promise to fire Police Superintendent Richard J. Brzeczek.   *(Lee Balterman)*

Most political experts considered the Hispanic vote up for grabs in the Epton-Washington contest. Here the Republican mayoral candidate dons a sombrero in the heart of Chicago's Mexican community at 18th and Blue Island Avenue. In the background his supporters shouted "viva Epton." *(Chicago Sun-Times)*

Influential and powerful Democratic party leader Edmund Kelly switched his support after the primary to Republican mayoral candidate Bernard E. Epton, whom he is introducing here to an audience. *(Lee Balterman)*

Mayor Jane Byrne pitched her appeal to the ethnic communities during the primary. Pictured above, Byrne received the endorsement of the Polish newspaper, *Dziennik Zwiazkowy*. To her right is 41st Ward Alderman Roman Pucinski, with Budget Director Anthony Fratto in the center and black alderman Wilson Frost to the left.   *(Chicago* Sun-Times*)*

Chicago's first female mayor, Jane Byrne actively sought the woman's vote during the primary. Here an energetic Byrne spoke before a large crowd in her upper middle-income home neighborhood, Sauganash on the city's Northwest Side.   *(Chicago* Sun-Times*)*

Mayor Jane Byrne gingerly greeting one of her opponents, Harold Washington, prior to the first Democratic primary debate. *(Chicago* Sun-Times*)*

Two weeks before the February 22 mayoral primary election, Washington's campaign gathered a new momentum following a massive rally at the University of Illinois Chicago Pavilion. 12,000 people heard speeches by the Reverend Jesse Jackson (left) and Democratic presidential aspirant Allan Cranston (right). On the far left is Washington campaign manager, Al Raby, a 1960s civil rights activist. *(Chicago* Sun-Times*)*

Former Vice President Walter Mondale endorsed Richard M. Daley during the primary. Mayor Jane Byrne countered with a letter of support from Massachusetts Senator Edward Kennedy. *(Chicago Sun-Times)*

In the primary campaign State's Attorney Richard M. Daley wrongly believed that he could garner a sizable portion of the city's black vote. Daley is seen here leaving a breakfast meeting after receiving the endorsements of seventy-five black ministers. The looming electoral disaster facing white candidates among black voters is captured in the angry protest signs of black pickets chastising their clergy for not supporting a fellow black, Harold Washington. *(Chicago Sun-Times)*

During the last week of the mayoral general election Harold Washington campaigned heavily in the independent, liberal lakefront wards. Many voters there were considered undecided, and the Democratic nominee knew he had to carry a sizable bloc to win. Pictured is a Washington supporter who revealed what many Chicagoans thought: the campaign had "gone to the dogs." *(Chicago Sun-Times)*

which of a variety of factors provided the narrow margin of victory. It may well have been the media. But it may also have been any number of other factors, such as the voter registration drives in black neighborhoods, the boomerang effect of Vrdolyak's racial remarks, or the efforts and financial resources of suburbanites and national Democratic figures that aided the Washington camp. We will never know for sure.

CONCLUSIONS: THE DEMOCRATIC DILEMMA

What major findings emerge from this exploration of media coverage of the 1983 Chicago mayoral race, and what is the larger significance of the election?

1) The Chicago media—including both print and electronic media—did a fine job in portraying the excitement of the election. The *Tribune* and *Sun-Times,* and to a lesser extent the *Defender,* also provided ample insights into the major policy issues and into the personal qualifications of all candidates. They put the election into the context of national party politics so that voters could grasp its impact on the Democratic and Republican parties.

2) The media did not do nearly as well in terms of balanced treatment of the candidates. They drew most information about Jane Byrne from hostile sources, while drawing most information about her opponents from friendly sources. In the case of Washington, there was hardly any scrutiny from anti-Washington sources. Fear of being accused of racism kept the media, as well as Washington's opponents in the primary election, from criticizing him or publicizing the views of his enemies. That this caution was wise was demonstrated during the general election: when Epton attacked his opponent's record, much of his criticism boomeranged because it was, indeed, labeled "racist."

3) The media also failed to discuss candidates along similar dimensions, making comparisons difficult. During the primaries, the greatest amount of coverage went to Jane Byrne, while Bernard Epton was largely ignored. During the general election campaign, Epton was no longer ignored, but he was definitely slighted. Moreover, the proportions of coverage devoted to various types of themes varied from candidate to candidate so that it was difficult to compare them in various policy areas. The media emphasized the incumbent's past performance, but did not give equal scrutiny to the performance records of her challengers. Imbalances resulted from journalistic choices rather than the nature of available news. This becomes clear

79

from comparisons of coverage in the three newspapers, where areas of deficiencies in one paper frequently are areas of ample coverage in another.

4) When it came to creating candidate images, the media refrained from using stereotypes based on family ties, gender, and religion. They also abstained from racial stereotypes with one major and highly unfortunate exception: that was the excessive emphasis on race as an issue, based on the assumption that a political contest between people of different races will nearly always be decided on the grounds of intraracial solidarity and interracial biases. There is evidence that racial cleavages can be bridged but that constant allegations about racial antagonisms may become self-fulfilling prophecies.

5) The campaign is also notable for a number of things that did *not* happen. The candidates who spent the most money on media advertising in the primaries did not win. Jane Byrne reputedly spent $1.6 million on television commercials and was frequently accused of buying the election. Some of her commercials were aired sixty-five to seventy times during the campaign, which presumably made them highly persuasive. Still, she lost in the primary. By comparison with Byrne, Richard Daley's expenses for commercials were modest at $900,000. And Washington's television commercials amounted to less than $200,000. Yet he turned out to be the winner. His campaign did benefit from radio commercials, especially the many on black radio stations urging their audiences to register and vote.[30] His concentration on voter turnout apparently paid off very well.

6) The election also demonstrated that major newspaper endorsements do not necessarily sway the voters in a contest where interest in the campaign runs high and voters learn much about the candidates. Both the *Tribune* and the *Sun-Times* endorsed Richard Daley during the primaries. Yet he came in last. However, it should be noted that the endorsement was weak. The *Tribune,* for instance, characterized Daley in its opening passages as the lesser of three evils. The editorial declared: "The prospect of four more years of Jane Byrne's roller-coaster administration or of getting on board the polarizing campaign of Rep. Harold Washington leaves The Tribune with no alternative but to endorse the election of Hizzoner's number one son, Richard Michael Daley, in the Feb. 22 Democratic primary."[31]

Despite its flaws, the coverage of the 1983 mayoral contest by Chicago's press was slightly above average, compared to the norm for other elections, when judged by the criteria we set out above. The public learned enough about the candidates to make choices intelligently. Still, democracy was not well served, and failure to defuse the racism issue is the reason. This failure has implications that reach beyond the Chicago situation.

Ours is the age of integration, the age in which major efforts are being made in many parts of the world to integrate diverse elements into the democratic body politic. In the United States we are seeing an increasing number of political contests in which population groups who have been hitherto absent from the political scene are making successful entries. Indeed, there is a black presidential candidate in 1984. Ways must be found to run such contests in the democratic tradition of free and open discourse so that voters can make decisions primarily on the merits of the contenders, rather than on the basis of media-fanned feelings of affinity with or dislike for people of a different heritage.

During the Chicago campaign there were no ground rules for covering a potentially inflammatory contest. Rather, there was a great deal of uncertainty about the kinds of issues that candidates and reporters may legitimately raise without earning the "racism" label. While Harold Washington, for instance, acknowledged that it was appropriate to discuss his legal problems, others called it racism on the grounds that many white politicians in the past had escaped similar scrutiny of their legal problems. A great deal of controversy swirled around an advertisement urging people to vote for Bernard Epton "before it's too late." Epton's campaign managers denied that the commercial was playing on racial fears, but Washington supporters insisted that it did. There were no guidelines to determine whether the slogan was inappropriate.

Questions also arose about the propriety of raising certain policy issues. For instance, was it racist fear-mongering when candidates and the media mentioned the issue of city housing policies when it entailed questions of locating poor black families in more affluent white neighborhoods? Should candidates and the media dwell on the race of public officials whose hiring or firing is discussed? Is it responsible for candidates to raise—and the media to publicize—the specter of racial hostilities in the wake of a hard-fought, dirty campaign? Obviously, such questions reveal major dilemmas for which ground rules need to be worked out.

The lessons of Chicago's campaign are that three major problems must be avoided in the future. One is the muzzling of critical debate when women and men from hitherto deprived groups enter the fray. The indiscriminate use of labels such as "racism" or "anti-feminism" or "anti-Semitism" is also a deterrent to open political debate and analysis. In Chicago, all candidates used the racism label deliberately to tarnish the reputation of opponents and to frighten them, to play on the emotions of people opposed to racism, and to garner attention from the media. The impact on open debate was stifling. Secondly, the media should avoid an undue emphasis on potentially stereotypical elements in an election. Washington should have been simply the candidate for mayor, not the *black* candidate—just as Jane Byrne was no longer referred to as the female mayor. It was also wrong to play up minor racial slips and to impute racism to millions of people on the basis of the bad behavior of a limited number of individuals. Finally, the Chicago campaign made it clear that ground rules for campaigning and for media coverage should be developed if harmony among racial and ethnic groups is the goal.

---

1. In the general election, Washington garnered 51.8 percent of the vote. This compares to 82.1 percent for Jane Byrne four years earlier, 77.4 percent for her predecessor, Michael Bilandic, and 77.7 percent for Richard Daley in his final election contest.

2. Thom Shanker and Douglas Frantz, "Epton Threatens to Sue Media, Flies to Florida," Chicago *Tribune,* April 14, 1983.

3. Coding categories were developed from the main themes of discussion in campaign stories, rather than from key words. Each theme was coded only once for each story, regardless of the number of repetitions. There was no limitation on the number of different themes which could be coded for a story. Reliability was checked according to the following formula: $R = 2Pab/Pa + Pb$, where R is reliability, Pa is the number of observations of the first coding, Pb is the number of observations of the second coding, and Pab is the number of agreed-upon observations. Intracoder reliability was 89 percent and intercoder reliability 84 percent, based on recoding of 10 percent of the stories. The greatest amount of discrepancy came in assessing the degree of favorableness of a story for a particular candidate. No category dropped below a 79 percent reliability rate. Individual categories contained from 3 to 30 coding options. Identification categories, such as date, newspaper name, and type of news story, were excluded from the computation because they inflate reliability scores unduly.

4. For a discussion of the features that make stories newsworthy, see Doris Graber, *Mass Media and American Politics* (Washington, D.C.: Congressional Quarterly Press, 1980), pp. 60-68; Dan Nimmo and James E. Combs, *Mediated Political Realities* (New York: Longman, 1983), pp. 48-70.

5. The role of personal qualities as criteria of choice is discussed by Gerald M. Pomper, with Susan S. Lederman, *Elections in America: Control and Influence in Democratic Politics* (2nd ed., New York: Longman, 1980), pp. 60-64; Jeffrey Smith, *American Presidential Elections: The Role of Trust* (New York: Praeger, 1980).

6. Thomas E. Patterson, *The Mass Media Election: How Americans Choose Their President* (New York: Praeger, 1980), p. 22.

7. The importance of "framing" in shaping public opinion is discussed in Shanto Iyengar, Mark D. Peters, and Donald Kinder, "Experimental Demonstrations of the 'Not-So-Minimal' Consequences of Television News Programs," *American Political Science Review*, 76:4 (Dec. 1982), 848-858. See also Wenmouth Williams, Jr., Mitchell Shapiro, and Craig Cutbirth, "Political Framing and Agenda Setting in the 1980 Presidential Campaign," 1982 ICA paper.

8. Examples are the 1980 presidential election, which dwelt on President Carter's "meanness," and congressional elections in 1982. Electronic mudslinging seems to be developing into a fine art.

9. Rick Soll, "Sawyer Still Stunned by Byrne Loss," *Sun-Times*, Apr. 3, 1983.

10. Michael J. Robinson, "The Media in 1980: Was the Message the Message?" in Austin Ranney, ed., *The American Elections of 1980* (Washington: American Enterprise Institute for Public Policy Research, 1981), p. 191.

11. *Sun-Times*, Feb. 9, 1983.

12. For discussion of media treatment of incumbents and front-runners, see Michael J. Robinson, "A Statesman is a Dead Politician: Candidate Images on Network News," pp. 159-186 in Elie Abel, ed., *What's News?* (San Francisco: Institute for Contemporary Studies, 1981).

13. Kathleen Whalen FitzGerald, "The Political Dynasty Hoax," Chicago *Tribune*, Jan. 30, 1983.

14. "Daley's the Best Hope," Chicago *Tribune*, Jan. 23, 1983.

15. David Axelrod, "Flurry of New Charges Hits Washington," Chicago *Tribune*, Apr. 7, 1983.

16. Barbara Brotman, "Washington Makes Plea for Support from Blacks," Chicago *Tribune*, Nov. 15, 1982.

17. Soll, *op. cit.*

18. Leanita McClain, "The Racial Truth of Politics," Chicago *Tribune*, Nov. 29, 1982.

19. In the general election, 18 percent of the whites voted for Washington, giving him "a bigger slice of the white vote than in similar black-white mayoral elections in all but one U.S. city." The one exception in a Northern city was Cleveland in 1967, when Carl Stokes received 20 percent of the white vote. Brian J. Kelly and Basil Talbott, Jr., "How White Vote Spelled Victory," *Sun-Times*, Apr. 14, 1983. Tom Bradley in Los Angeles exceeded these figures considerably.

20. Mitchell Locin and Douglas Frantz, "Byrne's Slip of the Tongue Causes Stir in Forum," Chicago *Tribune*, Jan. 29, 1983.

21. A fairly detailed account of the story is presented in Anne Keegan, "St. Pascal's Makes News—Hard Way," Chicago *Tribune*, Apr. 1, 1983.

22. "Is Race the Issue?" *Defender*, Mar. 2, 1983.

23. Anne Keegan, "Label of 'Racist' Overused, Abused," Chicago *Tribune*, Mar. 28, 1983.

24. Dennis Byrne, "Byrne Leading 2 Rivals in Poll," *Sun-Times*, Jan. 25, 1983.

25. Dennis Byrne and Sarah Snyder, "Washington Has White Support: Poll," *Sun-Times*, Feb. 25, 1983.

26. "Chicago Leaders Urge Civic Unity After First Black Mayor's Election," *New York Times*, Apr. 14, 1983.

27. Brian J. Kelly and Basil Talbott, Jr., "How White Vote Spelled Victory," *Sun-Times,* Apr. 14, 1983.

28. Dennis Byrne, "Images, Not Issues, May Sway Votes," *Sun-Times,* Feb. 20, 1983.

29. Byrne, cited in note 24.

30. Zay N. Smith, "Byrne Top TV Spender with $1.6 Million," *Sun-Times,* Feb. 21, 1983.

31. *Tribune, op. cit.,* n. 14.

V

Polling in the 1983 Chicago Mayoral Election

RICHARD DAY, JEFF ANDREASEN, and KURT BECKER

"When Alderman Edward Vrdolyak made his widely reported 'racist' appeal during a Northwest Side rally three days before the election ('A vote for Daley is a vote for Washington. . . . It's a racial thing. Don't kid yourselves') . . . Byrne's [black] support nosedived about seven points, most of which shifted to the Washington camp to ensure him a narrow victory."

—Richard Day

For years, Chicago politics has been dominated by forces other than voters. Mayors, kingpins, aldermen, committeemen, and financial moguls dominated the political turf. They decided who would be slated and ultimately who would hold office. The voters were a passive force. They were delivered. Politicos would proclaim (in the active voice), "I delivered my ward."

Corresponding to the rise of "the responsive voter,"[1] which Gerald Pomper has noted, the Chicago electorate from about 1976 on began to come alive. Candidates could actually make direct appeals to the electorate, and voters would respond. For example, in the Democratic primary in 1976, a pair of independent candidates running for the Illinois Supreme Court succeeded in defeating two candidates slated by then Mayor Richard J. Daley by making an appeal for quality justices on the bench. In 1979, Jane Byrne defeated the organization-backed Mayor Michael Bilandic with an appeal for efficient government, centering on a record-shattering snowfall.

As the political process in Chicago encompassed more participants, and campaigns became more competitive rather than pro forma, interest and turnout increased.

Because of the recent increases in voter turnout, the need to

TABLE I

Chicago Registrations and Voter Turnout in Key Elections from 1975 to Today

Year/Election	Chicago Voter Registration	Voter Turnout	Turnout as Percent of Registration
1975/Mayoral Primary	1,516,236	872,724	57.6%
1976/Presidential General	1,607,406	1,298,190	80.8%
1977/Mayoral Primary	1,613,258	759,136	47.1%
1979/Mayoral Primary	1,423,476	829,033	58.2%
1980/Presidential General	1,514,705	1,151,176	76.0%
1982/Governor's Race	1,549,084	998,106	64.4%
1983/Mayoral Primary	1,594,253	1,229,007	77.1%
1983/Mayoral General	1,625,786	1,332,703	82 %

"understand" these voters became important. Since the Democratic organization was less able to "deliver" a unified vote, it became more important to explore the dynamics of voter choice.

THE PRIMARY

Richard Day Research, Inc. (RDR) polled the Chicago Democratic primary electorate from early 1979 through early 1983. A survey question intended to measure the popular esteem for various public officials asks the voters to rank the candidates on a scale from zero through ten, where zero is the lowest and ten is the highest. Five is a neutral score.

Notice in Figure 1 below that Byrne's esteem score descended dramatically between the period when she assumed office and Sep-

POLLING DONE FOR THE PRIMARY

Polling Firm	Affiliate	Description of Surveying Done
Cambridge Survey Research	Harold Washington Campaign	One pre-election poll and one tracking poll
Dressner-Sykes	Jane Byrne Campaign	Over thirty surveys and daily tracking
William Hamilton and staff	Richard Daley Campaign	Two major surveys and weekly tracking for six weeks
Richard Day Research, Inc.	WLS-TV (ABC)	Two pre-election surveys
Gallup Organization	Chicago Sun-Times/ WMAQ-TV (NBC)	Two pre-election surveys
Market Facts, Inc.	Chicago Tribune	Six geographically stratified surveys
Market Shares	WBBM-TV (CBS)	Two pre-election surveys and exit poll

POLLING DONE FOR THE GENERAL

Polling Firm	Affiliate	Description of Surveying Done
Cambridge Survey Research	Harold Washington Campaign	Three pre-election polls and daily tracking
Market Opinion Research	Bernard Epton Campaign	One pre-election poll
Richard Day Research, Inc.	WLS-TV (ABC)	Three pre-election polls and exit poll
Gallup Organization	Chicago Sun-Times/ WMAQ-TV (NBC)	One pre-election poll
Market Shares	WBBM-TV (CBS)	Three pre-election surveys
WMAQ-TV (NBC)	WMAQ-TV/Associates Press	Exit poll
Market Shares	WBBM-TV (CBS)	Exit poll

tember 1982. Corresponding to Byrne's decline, esteem for Daley increased from a neutral rating in March 1979 to very strong ratings of 6.5 on the scale in the July 1981 and September 1982 surveys.

In a four-month span during late 1982 and early 1983, however, Byrne and Daley virtually traded places. The state's attorney moved from a very high rating downward to a point where he was rated

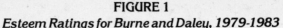

FIGURE 1
Esteem Ratings for Byrne and Daley, 1979-1983

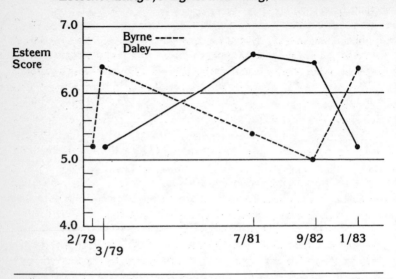

virtually neutral by the voters; Byrne, on the other hand, shot upward from a below-neutral position to one indicating high regard by the voters.

One reason for this shift came from Byrne's early media appeal to the Democratic voters. In the fall of 1982, Byrne urged Chicagoans to "Punch 10" (straight Democratic ticket) for the November 2 general elections. Daley announced his candidacy two days after the elections and promptly disappeared from public view. Byrne, on the other hand, launched a media blitz: her objective was to increase her low esteem by "re-educating" the voters. Through persuasive television and radio ads she admitted that she had made some mistakes; but she argued that Chicago was financially better off than it was when she took office, and furthermore that it took someone "tough and feisty" like her to run a tough city like Chicago. Byrne was virtually the only candidate on the air during the November and December campaign period.

Another reason for Daley's precipitous drop in the esteem rating is that in January he was being evaluated not as the state's attorney, but as a prospective mayor. RDR has on numerous occasions observed the phenomenon of a public figure being evaluated highly in his or her current office only to be severely downgraded when he or she runs for another one (e.g., Michael Howlett as secretary of state and Adlai Stevenson as a former U.S. Senator). In addition, as Byrne's side of the story was aired in her TV spots, the public perceived her as a more sympathetic figure and Daley merely as her challenger.

RDR polling in January 1983 showed the effect of Byrne's public re-education effort via the media. The poll asked voters not only for whom they would vote in the February 22 primary but why they would vote for that candidate. The two reasons most frequently mentioned by Byrne supporters were almost verbatim statements from her earlier ads: her past performance ("She has done a good job with the mess she started with . . . the city had a lot of financial problems, most of which have been straightened out . . ."; "Byrne came in on a mess . . . it takes time to straighten these things out. . . .") and her tough personality ("She's a fighter, she's got guts"; ". . . strong-willed, gets the job done"; ". . . straightforward, strong . . ."). Like a phoenix, she had risen from the ashes of low public esteem and was on course for a primary showdown.

The RDR and Gallup polls of late January 1983 reflect Byrne's rise in overall support among the city's electorate. Despite the entrance of Harold Washington as a third candidate, Jane Byrne held a significant lead over her opponents (see Table II). Support along racial lines had already emerged at this time, although not quite at the level it would later reach; Washington, for example, held a disappointingly low 44 percent of the black support at that time.

The incumbent Byrne had strong levels of support among whites (49%), blacks (32%), and Hispanics (53%). Because of her large support base with all racial groups, the two polls showed Byrne ahead of her opponents by a comfortable 15 to 19 percent in late January. Daley supporters, on the other hand, tended to be drawn from a narrow ethnic base of whites and Hispanics, for the black support he had once enjoyed was now divided between the other candidates. In fact, the RDR poll found Harold Washington virtually even with Daley in the polls.

TABLE II

Cross Tab of Race by Vote in Late January Poll (RDR)

Candidate Preference	White Percent	Black Percent	Hispanic Percent	All Groups Percent
Byrne	49%	32%	53%	41%
Washington	5%	44%	8%	22%
Daley	32%	7%	33%	21%
Undecided	14%	16%	6%	16%
				100%

February

As the primary neared, and as racial ties strengthened, Jane Byrne was slowly losing her support to her opponents. Washington simultaneously showed strong gains among the black electorate; in a few weeks his share of their support increased to 61 percent, and Byrne's support slipped seven points. This shift came mostly from the Southside, predominantly black wards.

Daley also cut into the mayor's electorate by extracting a substantial share of Her Honor's white support during the same period.

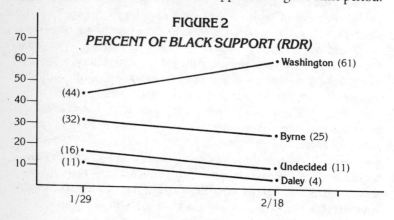

FIGURE 2
PERCENT OF BLACK SUPPORT (RDR)

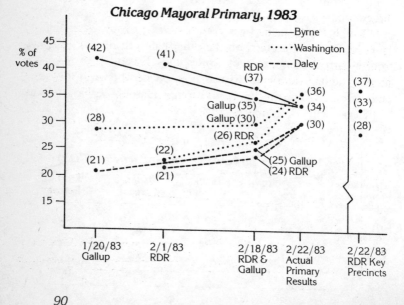

FIGURE 3
Chicago Mayoral Primary, 1983

As Byrne's share of the white vote skidded by six points, Daley's rose by seven, mostly from the Southside and Northwest wards. But even with those gains, Daley still trailed the mayor.

It is important to remember that Daley consistently ran last in almost every public opinion poll (RDR, Gallup, CSR, Dressner-Sykes). There is also reason to believe that his private professional polls showed the same. But the Daley campaigners vehemently denied this and conducted their own so-called "straw polls," which predictably showed him running first.[2] They feared being abandoned by voters who did not wish to support a loser and who would make Washington a winner. For despite Daley's gains among white voters (mostly from Daley country on the white South Side), these gains can only be described as modest compared to the groundswell of growing black support Washington was beginning to receive. And although Byrne's lead was being narrowed, it still seemed sufficient for victory. She still hung on to what appeared to be a winning share of white and Hispanic support and a solid 25 percent of the black vote. Her strongest support came from the predominantly white lakefront and Northwest wards, and the Latino region.

Four days before the primary, several polls (RDR, Gallup, Dressner-Sykes) found Byrne holding her lead between four and eleven percentage points over Washington. Daley was still running third with between 24 and 28 percent of the vote.

The Solidification of Support for Washington among Blacks

Race was never a stronger issue in the primary than it was during the final days of campaigning. The Byrne campaign realized that if she and Daley split the support of the white voting population, which makes up about 52 percent of Chicago's electorate, Washington had a good chance of winning if he cornered most of the black vote (which constitutes about 40 percent of the city electorate).

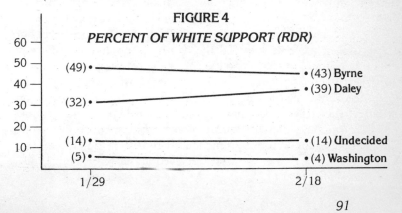

FIGURE 4

PERCENT OF WHITE SUPPORT (RDR)

	1/29	2/18	
Byrne	(49)	(43)	
Daley	(32)	(39)	
Undecided	(14)	(14)	
Washington	(5)	(4)	

TABLE III

Cross Tab of Area by Vote (RDR, 2/18)

Row	Byrne	Washington	Daley	Undecided	Row Total Percent
Lakefront	41%	16%	27%	16%	14%
Northwest, white	45%	5%	35%	15%	21%
Latino	47%	25%	16%	13%	7%
West Side, black	34%	37%	13%	16%	8%
South Side, black	25%	62%	5%	8%	23%
South Side, white	36%	15%	35%	14%	26%
Total Percent	37%	26%	24%	13%	n=622

Therefore, as a final desperate effort, the Byrne campaign approached Chicago white voters and urged them ". . . not to throw away their vote on Daley but to support Byrne as the best hope of keeping Washington out of the city."[3]

The Washington campaign staff apparently shared the belief that Washington could win with heavy black support, and they applied it to their strategy. The zeal for Washington among black voters during the last weekend and on the Monday before the primary was unprecedented: the city witnessed heavy campaigning by Washington and black mayors of other cities; long exhortations to vote for Washington on black-oriented radio stations; sermons from the pulpits of black churches on voting, coupled with prayer sessions (followed by "Get-Out-The-Vote" instructions) on the Monday evening before Election Day.

Unfortunately for Byrne, a calculated gamble in her own strategy reversed its intended effects and backfired. When Alderman Edward Vrdolyak made his widely reported "racist" appeal during a Northwest Side rally three days before the election ("A vote for Daley is a vote for Washington. . . . It's a racial thing. Don't kid yourselves."), most of Byrne's remaining black support jumped to the Washington camp. Nightly polling done by Dressner-Sykes during the final weeks recorded the damaging results on Byrne's re-election hopes of that impolitic appeal. Throughout the final week Byrne had maintained a strong lead over Washington, and it even appeared at one point that she could achieve a landslide victory. But the Dressner-Sykes poll measured the negative impact of Vrdolyak's statement (and the subsequent black mobilization efforts on her margin of support): during the final two days of the primary campaign Byrne's overall support nosedived about seven points, most of which shifted to the Washington camp to ensure him a narrow victory. It is not surprising that most of this shift in support was among black voters. According to the Associated Press exit poll, Washington gleaned an astonishing 93 percent of the black vote, which shows a 32 point increase in four days from RDR's latest preceding poll.

Key precinct analysis by RDR identified where in the city the three candidates ran best. Most of the late support for Harold Washington came from the South and West side, predominantly black wards. Byrne did especially well among voters in the lakefront-north, Latino, and northwest areas of the city. Finally, Daley corralled most of his votes from home turf in the Southside, predominantly white wards. Washington's long shot had paid off: the whites divided inconclusively between his two opponents.

THE GENERAL ELECTION

In the general election the question would be: could a city in which 78 percent of the voters call themselves Democrats elect a Republican? Jane Byrne had won the general election of 1979 with approximately 82 percent of the vote. Could Washington repeat that feat in 1983?

Harold Washington, with overwhelming black support (approximately 39 percent of the city electorate) would need white votes. On the heels of his primary victory, stories of his past legal

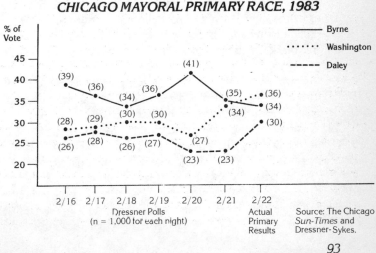

FIGURE 5

CHICAGO MAYORAL PRIMARY RACE, 1983

% of Vote

Byrne
Washington
Daley

45 —
40 — (39) (41)
(36) (36)
35 — (34) (35) (36)
(30) (30) (34) (34)
30 — (28) (29) (30)
(27)
25 — (26) (28) (26) (27) (27)
(23) (23)
20 —

2/16 2/17 2/18 2/19 2/20 2/21 2/22

Dressner Polls
(n = 1,000 for each night)

Actual
Primary
Results

Source: The Chicago
Sun-Times and
Dressner-Sykes.

93

problems began to receive maximum play. His virtually unknown opponent, Bernard Epton, would need to be taken seriously. It would certainly not be an "automatic" victory for the Democratic candidate, as it had been during the party machine's tenure. Race and each candidate's past became much more important than were their specific plans for the city. Polling conducted in the middle of March by RDR showed that race was still a strong indicator of voter sentiment, especially among blacks. Washington, at this time, carried 86 percent of the black support over from the primary.

By mid-March, Bernard Epton had had only nominal success in generating white support. Almost as many white voters said they were undecided (37 percent) as offered support to the Epton camp (39 percent). His most dramatic margins came from the Northwest and Southwest, predominantly white wards and from those who had previously voted for either Jane Byrne or Richard Daley in the primary.

Since nearly nine out of ten blacks had already made up their minds to support Washington, those who were undecided tended to be white voters. This portion of the electorate was cross-pressured: life-long white Democrats found it hard to vote for a Republican, but at the same time were hesitant about voting for a black Democrat for mayor. At that time, 24 percent of the white voters said they would vote for Washington.

By the end of March, however, the Epton campaign had been successful in helping white voters make up their minds. The direction of his strategy had concentrated on Washington's past legal problems, specifically his failure to pay his income taxes. These charges were heavily publicized by the media, which also dug up a few accusations of its own: Washington's delinquent utility bills and his actions in landlord-tenant disputes. Whites now had reasons not to vote for the black candidate—reasons which were not necessarily dependent on race.

In just two weeks between the March 15 and March 29 RDR surveys, Epton's support increased 11 percent. The gains came disproportionately from the Northwest white wards.

Black voters, on the other hand, seemed to ignore the Republican's charges. During this same period, black support for Washington actually increased by six points, which helped cushion the potential damage of his opponent's campaign. Eighteen percent of the whites stuck with Washington; he lost only 3 percent in the overall standings. Among all voters, Washington's decline was fairly small. The major finding underscores the fact that the publicizing

TABLE IV
Overall Frequencies

	3/15/83	3/29/83	Change in Percent
Washington	51%	48%	− 3%
Epton	23%	34%	+11%
Undecided	26%	18%	− 8%

FIGURE 6
Chicago Mayoral General Election, 1983

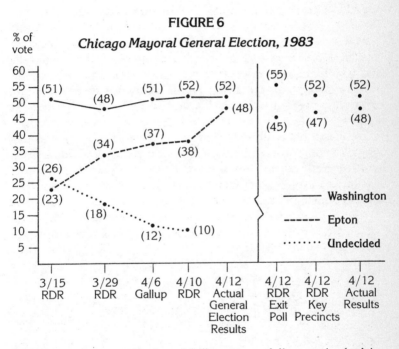

of Washington's tax, legal, and bill payment delinquencies had its biggest impact on undecided voters, a sizable segment who began to choose Epton.

The End of the Epton Campaign

As election day drew near, it seemed as though Washington's vote "hemorrhaging" had stopped as he regained the portion of the electorate he had previously lost. Table V reports shifts between the candidates during the general election among subgroups of the Chicago electorate. Epton increased his position largely by drawing the undecided voters to his corner. This effect was most pronounced among whites and in predominantly white areas (Northwest and

Southside wards). And Epton made steady inroads into Washington's support in the lakefront region.

Washington, on the other hand, retained his dynamic margins in the black areas of the city and even enlarged upon them. He coupled that base with a persistent share of roughly 20 percent of the whites (even on the Northwest Side and in the predominantly white areas of the South Side). Washington's gains among the Hispanic population of the city stemmed from the conversion of those who were previously undecided. Although the cell sizes are small, there is evidence in the RDR data of a shift among Latinos in the last two weeks of the campaign. With only a few days left before the election, it appeared that the contest could be close, especially if the undecided voters continued to move toward Epton.

At this point, the Epton campaign seemed to dwindle, and with three days left before the election, Epton almost dropped out of sight. The campaign's efforts became less directed and focused. Washington, on the other hand, saw two remaining areas for gaining support: the Hispanic and lakefront wards. With heavy campaigning in these areas, Washington was able to slow his losses on the lakefront and recapture lost ground among Latinos. In the closing days of the campaign, Washington promised that he would appoint a Hispanic deputy mayor and would establish an office of Hispanic affairs in city government. He had already promised reform to the lakefront.

Election Day

Exit polling was provided for two of the local television stations (ABC-TV and NBC-TV) by Richard Day Research, Inc. Voters were systematically asked to fill out a brief and confidential questionnaire after they had voted at their polling place. These results were called in, and RDR could then analyze actual voting patterns. The citywide poll for ABC-TV included 2,627 respondents, the NBC-TV poll 2,919.

In its exit poll for WLS-TV, RDR purposely oversampled in white areas of the city (specifically the lakefront north and southwest wards) to get a closer look at how these disproportionately white areas were voting. RDR also oversampled in the predominantly Latino wards. Conversely, the Southside and Westside black areas were undersampled because of the almost universal support for Washington in those wards. These returns were then weighted to bring the demographics back to their true proportions of the city-wide vote.

TABLE V
Shifts in Support by Race Over Time (RDR)

	3/15/83	3/29/83	4/10/83
By Race:			
White			
Washington	25%	18%	20%
Epton	39	58	66
Undecided	37	25	14
Black			
Washington	86%	92%	93%
Epton	1	3	2
Undecided	13	5	5
Hispanic			
Washington	57%	51%	67%
Epton	19	22	26
Undecided	24	27	7
By Region:			
Lakefront, North			
Washington	50%	42%	36%
Epton	22	41	52
Undecided	28	17	12
Northwest, White			
Washington	21%	18%	19%
Epton	38	60	69
Undecided	41	23	12
Latino			
Washington	68%	41%	81%
Epton	12	41	13
Undecided	20	19	6
West Side, Black			
Washington	82%	66%	87%
Epton	3	10	11
Undecided	15	24	2
South Side, Black			
Washington	83%	87%	88%
Epton	2	4	6
Undecided	15	9	6
South Side, White			
Washington	21%	28%	21%
Epton	46	50	60
Undecided	33	22	19

TABLE VI
Overall Frequencies

Candidate Preference	3/29/83	4/10/83	Change in Percent
Washington	48%	52%	+4%
Epton	34%	38%	+4%
Undecided	18%	10%	−8%

Table VII

Exit Polling of 1983 Mayoral General Election (RDR)

Washington %	(A) exit poll	(B) Closer area weights, refusals assigned exit poll adjusted	(C) Key precincts	(D) Assoc. Press exit poll	(E) Actual election results
Citywide	54.8	54.0	52.3		51.8
Area					
Lakefront North	44.7	50.5	38.6		38.4
Northwest white	16.9	16.1	13.2		12.3
Latino	57.5	58.1	53.6		50.0
West and South black	94.9	94.0	94.1		94.1
South white	23.4	23.4	22.1		24.2
Race					
White	17.1	17.5		18	
Black	98.8	98.9		98	
Hispanic	67.9	72.4	x		x
Other	33.3	34.9			
Age					
18-27	62.4	62.8		(18-24) 61	
28-35	65.5	65.0		(25-34) 60	
36-49	54.2	55.0	x	(35-49) 55	x
50-59	42.3	41.8		(50-64) 34	
60+	26.3	25.6		(65+) 30	
Sex					
Male	52.6	52.0		54	
Female	54.7	53.7	x	51	x

Based on the data received from this poll, RDR was able to give its first prediction to the ABC-TV news team at 7:01 p.m.: Harold Washington would win with 55 percent of the vote. About this time, CBS-TV said that while things looked good for Washington, Epton might still win. And NBC-TV simply said the race was too close to call.

RDR also used actual returns from those precincts that have historically reflected overall voting patterns in order to determine the winner early in the evening. These "key" precincts showed that while RDR's earlier prediction was a little high (due largely to misreporting in the lakefront north wards), Washington would still win with 52 percent of the vote.

The exit poll data proved a remarkably good indicator of the Washington victory as it was building. Unlike in the earlier elections of 1982 and 1980, the exit polls came within tenths of a percentage point in divining the final result. The exit polls not only correctly predicted the result but also gave psephologists and veteran election watchers a sophisticated breakdown of voter demographics which the raw election results could not. The demographics of the exits also showed that gender seemed to make little difference in the end, but race, Hispanic origins, age, and region of the city did count for something. The falling off of the Washington vote—from a high of 65 percent among the twenty-eight to thirty-five-year-olds to a low of 26 percent among the sixty-year-olds plus—reflects the age structure of blacks and whites in Chicago. Blacks are very youthful, with a low median age, whereas whites conversely are heavily beyond their childbearing years and with a high median age. Just as age was a mirror of race, so too was region. The white Northwest and South-west sides offered Washington his lowest support levels, whereas lakefront liberals, either true to their ideologies or with guilt-ridden consciences, saw the black standard-bearer as the best candidate. Blacks were overwhelmingly attracted to Washington, demonstrating a loyalty by race that Epton could not match with his white supporters.

CONCLUSION

During the 1983 election season, the public opinion polls conducted by the news media played an important role by keeping the candidates' "insider" polls honest and reporting these results openly to the public. Without them, only the "insider" polls, subject to manipulation by the candidates, would have kept track of the campaign vicissitudes as reflected in public opinion.

The major polls showed the incredible volatility of the Chicago electorate and how the political fortunes of various candidates could rise and fall in shockingly short periods of time. Richard M. Daley came through most of 1982 riding a high wave of public esteem and promising bits of reform, or at least restoration, and to rescue his father's beloved city from the clutches of the intruder of the Northwest. Jane Byrne, under the adroit professional grooming of media consultant David Sawyer, rose like a phoenix from the ashes of low public esteem to lead the polls until the eve of the primary election. Richard Daley's campaign and public esteem ratings stalled in neutral in December. Newspaper columnists and the Byrne camp derided Daley for not being able to speak his mind on the issues, and one popular columnist called him "chicken." This baiting worked, for Daley entered the debates and, to the pleasant surprise of his supporters, took the negative edge off the widespread rumor that he could not stand on his feet and debate at the same time. Speech lessons at Northwestern had undoubtedly improved his delivery; but they did not do much for his standing in the polls. As the public opinion polls showed, nothing seemed able to resuscitate Daley's sinking campaign, for he never improved his position from December 1982 onward. His endorsements by major newspapers may have nudged a few points his way, but not enough to win and only at Byrne's expense.

The Byrne strategists perhaps realized too late that their real opponent was Washington; for when they tried to capitalize on that fact, they were labeled racists and probably lost the primary on that misfired stratagem. Washington's staff, although often in confusion, deftly exploited this tactical blunder of his opponents and headed them off at the pass in the grey dawn of election morn. As Figure 5 shows, the Harold Washington forces broke through the Byrne lines on the public opinion charts at the very last moment and closed the gap and snatched victory on election day. Without the public opinion polls, Chicagoans would not have been able to track this intriguing drama with the precision of generals mapping a campaign.

The general election that followed between Democrat Washington and Republican Epton provided fewer surprises to pollsters, but it was still important to track because of the mass partisan defection in the primary, which looked as though it could be repeated in the general election. That proved to be the case. Washington won what Chicagoans called a "squeaker" on April 12, and RDR, with its sample precincts and some actual returns, predicted that result early on election night. The polls gave us a valuable tool for measuring the salience or nonsalience of issues such as the candidate's record, gender, race, and partisan loyalty in one of Chicago's truly historic and memorable elections. As the Chicago electorate becomes more fragmented, and as candidates begin to appeal to discrete and often contradictory interest groups within the Democratic party structure, public opinion polling will increasingly become an important tool for understanding what may be a new Byzantine Windy City polity.

1. Gerald Pomper, *Voter's Choice* (New York, 1970).

2. To this day, Daley campaign staff members blame the public opinion polls for their candidate's loss and not their own faltering campaign efforts or those of their candidate or the political adeptness of Richard Daley's two opponents.

3. Paul M. Green, *Illinois Issues* (April 1983), 19.

VI

How the 1983 Mayoral Election Was Won: Reform, Racism, and Rebellion

DON ROSE

"It was a campaign cliche to say that a black candidate other than Washington might have had an easier time winning; but it is also safe to say that a white candidate other than Epton, running a less strident campaign, might have wound up mayor."

—Don Rose

No one doubts that it was the dirtiest, most bizarre, and perhaps most inept major political campaign ever witnessed on a citywide scale in this most political of all American cities. No one doubts that the choice of major candidates was the strangest ever offered to Chicago voters. From the moment the winner of the Democratic primary election became clear, matching him up with the then perfunctory Republican, the streets of Chicago crackled and cackled that the choice was between a "sheenie and a shine."

Indelicate as the quip may be, it was a fairly accurate reflection of the majority views of white ethnic Chicago, one that would be reflected again in the final breakdown of the votes on election day. It was one of those elections that really told more about the electorate's social attitudes than its political views. Although many issues were implied, including those of political reform, party loyalty, and fiscal integrity, there seems little doubt that racial attitudes were the dominant factors in the end.

But the campaign that would bring Chicago its first black mayor ever—and its first reform mayor in some three decades—was as notable for its eccentricities as for its historical import. The Democrat, enigmatic even to his friends, was a political maverick who had served time in jail and had been suspended from the bar; the Republican was a kind of maverick as well, with a reputation for an explosive temper and sarcastic wisecracking.

101

Not only were there the unique and colorful backgrounds and personalities of the two candidates; there was also the brief intrusion of an abortive write-in campaign by the incumbent—herself an unusual personality—who had been defeated in a primary election nearly as strange as the general election that would follow it.

It was earmarked as well by the defection of a significant number of Democratic party officials and aldermanic candidates, by the remarkable entry into a local race of a herd of national Democratic party officials—including most of the avowed presidential candidates—and by national and international media coverage on a day-to-day basis comparable only to a presidential contest. On top of it all, it turned out to be the most expensive local political campaign in the recorded history of the world.

"Harold Washington had become the darling of Chicago's independent-liberal community—or at least that part of it represented by the Independent Voters of Illinois-Independent Precinct Organization—in the course of the special mayoral election of June 1977, called to fill the unexpired term of Richard J. Daley, who had died the previous December. The alliance between Washington and the organized white independents came about only after an internal organizational struggle had taken place based on questions about whether this established creature of the Chicago political machine was truly committed to independence and reform, or whether his challenge to Michael Bilandic, the acting mayor, was simply an ethnic power play. "

Washington's conviction for failure to file income tax returns for four years, and his brief suspension from the bar for failing to serve clients, did not sit very well with many of the reform-minded lawyers in the organization; but the militants within the group won the day with a significant vote of endorsement.

The course of that 1977 primary campaign convinced not only the doubting IVI-IPO, but turned Washington into the city's major black political leader, despite the fact that he carried only a third of the black wards and gained a mere 11 percent of the total vote. Militant black community leaders who participated in the campaign, including commentator-columnist Lu Palmer and police organizer Renault Robinson, would become the nucleus of the drive in early 1982 to register black voters and run a major campaign for a black mayor in 1983.

Washington's standing as a folk hero began to build in the primary election of 1978, when he was officially reslated to run for his mid-Southside state senate seat. But enemies within the Democratic party itself, presumably with the tacit approval of Mayor Michael Bilandic, worked vigorously against him. Hoping to confuse the voters, they put two other candidates named Washington on the same ballot, but he managed to remove one of them on a technicality.

Washington won that primary by a handful of votes but came out of it convinced that he no longer had a future with the party. The next year, he decided to run for the First District Congressional seat once held by his late mentor, Ralph Metcalfe. That district had far more independent voters than did his senate district; it included the white liberal constituency centered in the Hyde Park-University of Chicago community and the far Southside, middle-income black wards he carried in the 1977 race.

The incumbent was Bennett Stewart, committeeman of the 21st Ward, who was named to replace the deceased Metcalfe scant months before the 1978 general election. Also in the race was John Stroger, Democratic committeeman of the Eighth Ward, who had never bucked the party before. Finally, Ralph Metcalfe, Jr., son of the late congressman, entered to claim what he saw as the family heritage, while other independents saw only the potential for fatally splitting the district's independent vote.

As it turned out, their fears were unwarranted, for Washington gained just short of half the vote, while the others split the balance, the two machine candidates coming in third and fourth. With his position now secure, Washington moved into Hyde Park (only a few short blocks away from Republican State Representative Bernard Epton), built a strong progressive-liberal record in the U.S. Congress, and enhanced his home base to the point where the regulars did not even oppose him in the 1982 congressional primary. That decision came in part because they felt he could not be defeated, and in part because the machine did not want to suffer any divisive battles that year. They hoped that no one would rock the black part of the boat those few months before Mayor Byrne was to seek re-election.

They miscalculated.

The machine was not really used to losing big primaries, despite the debacle of 1979, which brought them Mayor Jane Byrne, or the subsequent debacle of 1980, which brought them State's Attorney Richard M. Daley, Supreme Court Justice Seymour Simon, Congressman Gus Savage, and Congressman Harold Washington.

103

And even after most of those defeats—especially after the Byrne primary—it was still expected that some form of rapport would be reached between the victorious primary challengers and the party regulars.

Byrne became one with the old guard of the party almost instantly after her primary. Simon stayed with his judicial reform issues and picked no further internal battles. Daley worked hard to rebuild relationships with the party and would have succeeded, but Byrne saw him as a threat and tried to defeat him in the general election. Once in office, however, his pledges to prosecute governmental miscreancy never materialized. Even Washington and Savage played it reasonably cool with the party during the general election campaigns of 1980 and 1982, though they were not team players in the Illinois Democratic congressional delegation.

But a strange thing happened in the immediate wake of Washington's primary victory: he failed to come to the party to seek rapport and favor. He had the temerity to wait for the committeemen to come to him. As he put it in a succinct aside, "I'm not going to kiss their asses."

Worse yet, he issued ultimatums to the effect that all good Democrats had to support him if they were to be considered Democrats at all. He threatened to help defeat all Democrat candidates in the 1984 elections if the regulars did not support him; and his campaign manager, Al Raby, called for the replacement of Edward R. Vrdolyak as chairman of the party. Vrdolyak, for his part, quickly began issuing worried statements to the effect that Washington actually might lose the general election. Ironically, during the primary he had uttered fears that Washington might win. His statements were evidence to the Washington forces of a ploy aimed at scaring them back into a relationship of some kind with the regulars. Not only was a made-in-heaven marriage not in the offing, but a good shotgun ceremony was equally unlikely.

A major defector from the Democratic ranks, Alderman Roman R. Pucinski (41st Ward), said in a television interview justifying his move: "You expect to hear a lot of antimachine rhetoric in a primary. But it's not supposed to go on after you win. Here's this guy threatening to destroy us." Pucinski might well know about antimachine rhetoric: he ran as an independent in the 1977 primary against Bilandic and Washington. But he had no problems coming back into the fold and behaving himself thereafter.

This Washington, though, was a horse of a different color.

There might have been no Epton campaign at all had it not been for Pat Quinn, the neopopulist reformer whose energies were directed at organizing referendum campaigns in Illinois after he left the administration of former Governor Dan Walker. Frustrated at almost every turn, he finally won a big one—a 1980 referendum to reduce the state house of representatives by one-third, create single-member house districts, and abolish cumulative voting. Up to that point the state would elect three representatives from each of fifty-nine districts, virtually always two from the majority party and one from the minority.

Bernie Epton, a successful insurance lawyer whose brother Saul was a respected Republican circuit court judge, became the minority GOP representative in the liberal, independent 24th District in the 1968 election. His fellows were Robert E. Mann, then dean of the independent liberals in the state house, and Lewis A. H. Caldwell, a black regular who paid occasional lip service to liberalism while in the Hyde Park precincts of this overwhelmingly black district. Caldwell's predecessor in the seat was the liberal saint Abner J. Mikva.

Epton seemed to fit well into the district—for a Republican. He was viewed as a liberal Republican, certainly not tied to the ultraconservative elements in his party, good especially on racial issues and the usual constellation of good-government and election reform issues favored by the IVI-IPO. He received IVI-IPO backing in his campaigns throughout the 1970s, though in the special circumstance of being a minority-party representative, with the existing GOP structure behind him, he never had a serious primary challenge nor a worrisome general election until 1978. In his legislative campaigns he was spared media scrutiny, political skirmishing, and the attacks of a worthy opponent.

He was high-strung and often eccentric during his fourteen years in public office, and neither the press nor the public put him to any serious test as a public official. His most notable public gesture during his tenure was the release to the press of his belief that he had the highest IQ of any of his colleagues.

While he was not a perfect liberal (since he cast frequent conservative votes on economic issues—especially in the late 1970s and early 1980s), few in the district or in the media ever questioned his record. Later in the mayoral campaign, it would be noted that as an insurance-industry lawyer he had sat on the General Assembly's insurance committee and voted on matters that should have been considered conflicts of interest. A pro-utility record would also be traced, along with Republican party-line votes such as those retaining the sales tax on food and medicine.

Mann retired before the 1978 Democratic primary, and two Hyde Park-type independents sought his seat. Strangely enough, both Carol Moseley-Braun, a black, and Barbara Flynn Currie, a white, won—ousting Caldwell. It was the first time ever that independents took two seats in a district. But Caldwell did not give up; he mounted an independent campaign in the general election on a third-party line, with Epton as his target.

Epton was forced to run a high-gear campaign for the first time in his political career. But even that was not very tough, for he had a lot of money plus the support of IVI-IPO and all the major media. There were also enough white votes in the district to elect him, using the cumulative "bullet" vote, which tripled a voter's effectiveness. He beat Caldwell handily, though only a small portion of the district's voters were involved; the rest voted Democratic.

There are those today, including this writer, who believe that Epton's frequent fulminations and explosions against the media and many of his former IVI-IPO-type supporters during the mayoral campaign stemmed from the fact that he had never before had to campaign so vigorously, subject himself to ongoing media scrutiny, or otherwise engage in the rough and tumble of Chicago politics. But it is almost certain that he would never have become a citywide candidate had the referendum creating single-member districts not unseated him from a sinecure. It was clear that he could never win his old seat back against a Democrat in a head-to-head contest—especially now that the district was more than 80 percent black.

Thus Bernie Epton moved out of Hyde Park and to the Gold Coast of the near North Side. When he let it be known, then, that he was available for a draft to become the GOP standard-bearer in the 1983 mayoral election, the reaction in political circles was that this was his last hurrah, a kind of ego trip and another of his eccentric moves. According to those closest to him, Epton thought that he would be running against Jane Byrne and the Ed Vrdolyak machine and that he would lead a charge of IVI-IPO liberals, disaffected blacks, and reformers, along with the city's closet-bound Republicans. He hoped to fight the good fight.

The mayoral campaign would demonstrate, however, that his move from racially integrated, liberal, genteel Hyde Park was more than geographic.

The last time anyone in Chicago had taken a Republican mayoral candidate seriously was in 1963, when a one-time Democrat and former state's attorney, Ben Adamowski, lost to Richard J. Daley by fewer than 150,000 votes. Even then, they didn't take Adamowski very seriously until after the election, when it turned out that Daley had lost the white vote.

The 1967 candidate was a Republican committeeman from the Southwest Side's 23rd Ward, a Polish-American named John Waner, who underperformed his own abilities and lost every ward. He came out looking like a clown.

Richard Friedman, another former Democrat, head of the Better Government Association and a former assistant Illinois attorney general, ran a very serious, issue-oriented race in 1971 and attracted the city's independent-liberal community. He never looked like a clown, but he only got 30 percent of the vote and carried only two wards. He wound up in Bernie Epton's law firm.

John Hoellen, last of the Republican aldermen, tried it in 1975. Stunts like driving a snake out of City Hall on St. Patrick's Day helped put him in the clown category, and he lost his 47th Ward aldermanic seat on the way, along with all the wards.

An honest-to-God professional clown named Ray Wardingley, who went by the professional name Spanky, threatened to become the GOP nominee in the 1977 special election. That was too much for the professionals in the party, who located the newest last-of-the-Republican aldermen, Dennis Block, a Jewish fellow who eked out a win in the 48th Ward with the support of independents—and a new candidate was born. Block wound up moving out to the suburbs and surrendering his aldermanic seat after losing all the wards in 1977.

Spanky Wardingley remained a threat in 1979, so the party located financier-businessman Wallace Johnson to run against the presumed Democratic primary winner, Michael Bilandic. The amiable Johnson took on the kamikaze mission as a gesture toward the party. He thought it was a good break that he wound up running against Jane Byrne, surprise winner of the primary, because he might be fighting a divided Democratic party—and there might be some folks willing to vote against a woman on general principles. Showing the traditional underperformance of those thrust into that position, Johnson had his photo taken with his sweater pulled up above his belly button, and he made comments about how men in the neighborhoods didn't want a woman mayor because females had menstrual periods.

The party wasn't divided after all, and no one seemed to care much one way or the other about menstrual cycles. Johnson got less than 18 percent of the vote, losing not only every ward but carrying only two precincts in the greatest rout in the modern history of mayoral politics.

Now came the third Jewish Republican mayoral candidate in little more than a decade—wealthy and liberal, with a beard to boot. Was it rout time again? Even Epton could make light of the situation, though he often expressed the view that he deserved at least a little media coverage. He complained that the cameras always turned off when he came up to the stand following any of the major Democratic contenders. He also complained bitterly of the absence of financial and other assistance from his party. In fact, the last time President Reagan spoke in Chicago, only a few months earlier, Epton was not even on the dais but in the back of the house on a ticket he had to purchase himself. But he knew the way the game was played, and he publicly acknowledged the kamikaze nature of his mission, except, of course, in the most unlikely case that "Harold" should win the primary. Nudge, nudge. Wink, wink. Titter, titter.

The nudging, winking, and tittering ended abruptly early on the morning of February 23rd. But even before the results were final, Epton was on the air vowing that race would never become the issue in his campaign. Yes, he knew there was bigotry in Chicago, but he would never exploit it, and he would fire anyone in his campaign caught using it. He also said, early on the morning after the primary, that he would not hire a media consultant and that he expected to run very few commercials.

But the party that had forsaken him in his lonely mission soon swung into gear. James Fletcher, the key political operative of Governor Jim Thompson and manager of his first gubernatorial victory, took over as Epton's manager. John Deardourff, of the nationally known GOP consulting firm of Bailey-Deardourff, took over as media director. Epton met with members of the Republican National Committee, who pledged support in the hundreds of thousands of dollars.

Local Republicans perked up. Here was a real chance at the mayor's seat at long last, for the obvious reason that the Democrat was black—and, of course, had not got much more than a third of the vote in the primary.

The new campaign would be aimed at "disaffected" Democrats, many of whom began to pour into Epton's office on the Wednesday morning after the primary. Even before a single Democratic committeeman or aldermanic runoff candidate came over to Epton, hundreds of Byrne and Daley volunteers—many of them public employees and party workers—had made the move.

At the same time, local GOP functionaries began working up plots to have Epton resign his candidacy and make way for a person with a higher vote-getting capability. Richard B. Ogilvie was a name on many lips, but the former governor denied interest. Democrats too, such as Jane Byrne and even Edward R. Vrdolyak, were interested in making the switch. But Epton, who had taken on the impossible mission for whatever personal gratification he found in it, was not about to surrender the chance to become Chicago's first Republican mayor since 1927. At the age of 61, he did not really want a lesser position, and with the millions he had made in his thriving law firm and a career of good investments, he could not be bought off.

"Mr. Epton has a chance to be mayor not because he is a Republican, or because he has outstanding qualifications, or because he has an unbeatable campaign organization. He is a legitimate contender for one reason only—because he is white and because the Democratic nominee, Rep. Harold Washington, is black," declared the Chicago *Tribune* on March 13, 1983, in a surprisingly early endorsement of Washington.

But the *Tribune* was only saying what everybody with the least bit of savvy knew and understood. It is what Cook County GOP Chairman J. Robert Barr knew and understood the weekend before the election, when he exhorted the candidate's new-found volunteers to go get out the vote any way they could—forget about the fancy charts and maps and campaign plans, just get out the vote. Everyone knew what this campaign was all about.

Everyone on the street knew instantly, and it didn't take Epton long to get into the swing of things. From his opening statement that "I do resent anyone who would vote for me because I'm white," he moved quickly to portraying himself as a victim of "reverse racism."

Washington, of course, saw the repetitious references to race, in any context, as a not so subtle reminder of the obvious. As Epton began to encounter cheering hordes, with their chants of "Ber-nie-Ber-nie-Ber-nie," a massive outpouring of love and adoration he had never experienced in his political career, he began to play to the crowds, giving them what they wanted. His earlier proclamations of respect for the intelligence and ability of his opponent gave way to attacks on Washington's intelligence. In one speech, while criticizing Washington for going to a fund-raiser in Washington, D.C., Epton said that the Democrat should "bring back some brains." Epton campaigned only in white communities and was stung when the issue was raised; but he could cite no black areas outside of Hyde Park where he had appeared. By March 11, Epton had stated a theme that he would reiterate many times with a few minor variations: "Harold [he always called him by his first name] in my opinion is not the best qualified candidate the black community can produce."

From that point forward, Epton speeches were peppered with references to Washington's "minority group" contrasted to "my minority group," which, he pointed out, would never put up a candidate with such a bad record. Epton also chose to keep bringing up the name of Jesse Jackson, who, campaign legend had it, would really run the city if Washington ever got in. One would think Jackson was the real opposition, the way Epton played it, though Washington was doing his best to keep Jackson out of camera range.

Of course, Epton never had to say much more than that, though in the final weeks he picked up a favorite issue in the white ethnic communities: he supported a questionable ordinance banning the posting of "For Sale" signs in front yards.

Meanwhile, his supporters were sporting T-shirts with sayings such as "Vote Right—Vote White." Epton's own slogan, flashed incessantly on television ads until the last week of the campaign—when public outcries finally forced it off the air—was only slightly more subtle: "Epton. Before it's too late."

Blacks had elected Jane Byrne in 1979. Now they had defeated her. It was all over so suddenly, so unexpectedly. There must be a way around it. But it was too late to petition for an independent line on the ballot. Maybe Epton could be got off the ballot. If that didn't work, maybe get the Socialist Workers party line. Perhaps they could be bought. (Later, the SWP said someone did try to buy the ballot line—some Rush Street characters, one a suburbanite, presumed to be representing Byrne.)

A write-in was the last resort, since Epton could not be talked off the ballot or bought off. Those crazy socialists couldn't be bought off either, not even for a million dollars. So Byrne announced the write-in effort, which had been hinted at just after the primary, on March 15. Lunacy? Not in the context of Chicago's racial politics—and everyone understood that. Suddenly the write-in campaign was in the newsweeklies and the national press.

Most of Byrne's primary campaign staff was against the idea, including campaign manager Bill Griffin. Few staffers other than aide Nancy Philippi and media hand Pat Fahey remained. Husbandadvisor Jay McMullen also remained. Fund-raiser Thomas King, head of the Kennedy-family-owned Merchandise Mart was on board, then off quickly upon orders from the Kennedy family. David Sawyer, the media wizard who had brought Byrne back from the political dead in November only to have her die again in February, was on board. Then the Democratic National Committee threatened to blacklist him as a consultant, and he jumped off. Multimillionaire real estate developer Miles Berger and his wife Sally, both beneficiaries of Byrne largesse during her tenure, stayed on.

Neither the Kennedys nor the DNC wanted to be associated with a campaign that was outside the Democratic party and based on race. Byrne, you see, was developing her own code words. In her opening statement and in interviews and speeches she said she was mounting this near-impossible campaign because the city was still too "fragile" to be entrusted to anyone else. It could, she said, "go up" or "slip back."

Epton denounced her. Washington denounced her. Daley denounced her. The newspaper and television editorialists denounced her. It would clearly split the Epton vote, so none of his supporters, including already defected ward committeemen, would move to her.

Washington strategists secretly liked the idea: a split in the anti-Washington forces would make their lot easier, as happened in the primary. The down-side for them was that they had to go back to the drawing boards for their TV campaign strategy: just who was the clearest political threat? how should they handle it? The delay was getting costly.

To mount a write-in campaign successfully, the Byrne campaign would have to undertake a massive education campaign, which was happening in the media already. They explained that one had to write in the name of the office on the little Vote-a-Matic envelope, then make a box and put in an X, and then, finally, the candidate's name. Stickers and rubber stamps could not be used; there was already case law against it.

But perhaps the election board could be petitioned to preprint a place for write-ins. The board's answer was no. Then the circuit court said no again. A week after the announcement of the campaign, despite earlier protestations that she would carry on regardless of what the courts said, Jane Byrne threw in the towel.

It was a hell of a week. Byrne said afterward that she was a Democrat: it was her way of saying that she was not backing Epton. It was also her way of saying she would do nothing for Washington.

But then, neither would Daley, who had actually endorsed him formally.

Racial politics was nothing new to Ed Vrdolyak. He first won election as ward committeeman in 1968, running as an insurgent, by suing the city to prevent a school busing plan from touching his neighborhood. The East Side, where he came from and stayed, is a racially conservative, white ethnic enclave. Racial change there means more Croatians are coming in.

Martin Luther King had marched there in 1966. More than a decade earlier, Eastsiders had been more than active in the Trumbull Park race riots in the adjacent neighborhood, where violence raged for nearly five years because blacks moved into a public housing project. Racial violence also flared regularly at the East Side's Calumet Park beach, when an occasional black had the nerve to try to swim in the public waters.

Going against the party was nothing new for "Fast Eddie" either. In 1972 he supported Richard M. Nixon for president against George McGovern. In 1974 he ran in the primary against the slated Democratic candidate for assessor. He lost badly, but it was like Japan losing World War II: he did very well thereafter.

Vrdolyak's ability to retain peaceful control of the 10th Ward, with its white ethnics, blacks, and Mexicans living adjacent to each other in hostile camps, is testimony to his political skill. As party chairman, following a bruising battle he and Byrne waged against incumbent George Dunne, he was being applauded for almost getting Adlai Stevenson elected governor. His next big triumph was to be the renomination of Jane Byrne.

Sensing that Byrne was slipping, Vrdolyak made a speech to party loyalists the weekend before the primary election, stating baldly that the race was about race. A vote for Daley would be a vote for Washington and against the way things were supposed to be, he said. A vote for Byrne was the only way to keep things right and white. Unfortunately for him, a few reporters whom he did not recognize were in the audience—one from the Chicago *Tribune*, one from the Kansas City *Times*, and a nationally syndicated columnist who appears in the *Sun-Times*. Some people credit and some blame the speech for Washington's victory. It surely didn't hurt his cause, though that may not be what actually killed off Daley.

After the primary, Vrdolyak publicly gritted his teeth and endorsed Washington; but the endorsement, personal and later on behalf of the party, didn't mean much. His own precinct captains in the white sectors of his ward were already going for Epton. He also donated money to a rump organization in the 26th Ward that was openly working for Epton. He announced that Washington could easily lose, and he showed Washington a "survey" that indicated a 30,000-vote defeat. That's not the way a party leader is supposed to talk. But the party below him was not acting much like a party should either.

Committeeman Edmund Kelly of the North Side 47th Ward, not known for its liberal racial views, was out trying to organize committeemen for Epton days after the primary. As head of the Park District, Kelly knew his days would be numbered if Washington won. Byrne once almost did him in, but there would be no kissing and making up with this reformer. It wasn't just that Washington was a reformer; it was also important that the Park District was under constant siege in the courts and in the press for racial discrimination.

Meanwhile, Aloysius Majerczyk, the maverick alderman of the 12th Ward on the Southwest Side who was engaged in a tight runoff election with the ward committeeman, Theodore Swinarski, endorsed Epton. A policeman, Majerczyk said race had nothing to do with it; it was a matter of "law and order." Days later, another policeman, Ivan Rittenberg, machine alderman of the Northwest Side 40th Ward, did the same. Other white runoff candidates would follow.

Vito Marzullo, dean of the old-line aldermen and committeemen, salty and outspoken racially—who called his 25th Ward Mexican opponents "wetbacks"—was an early defector. He invited Epton to address his annual fund-raiser and received a godfatherly kiss on the cheek from the Republican candidate. Well, Marzullo once backed Nixon also.

Eventually, eight ward committeemen, most from white ethnic Northwest and Southwest Side wards, would formally endorse Epton. Roman Pucinski, who first indicated he would go with the winner of the primary election on principle, was the last of the committeemen to defect publicly. Many more stayed "neutral." Most of them stayed away from the Pyrrhic endorsement session finally called by Vrdolyak, although some sent representatives. All in all, it was not the kind of session a forceful party chieftain could be proud of. Neither was the final election result.

It was easy to figure out that the campaign's battleground was going to be the north lakefront: wards 42, 43, 44, 46, 48, 49, and, to a more limited extent, 50. This was independent turf, where voters had split tickets in general elections, voted for insurgent Democrats in primaries, and elected two or three antimachine aldermen in elections throughout the 1970s. The cliche described the voters as "lakefront liberals," but that was too glib. Certainly the voters were reform-oriented, and they paid more attention to newspaper endorsements than did those in other parts of the city. But many were Republicans, although they were not especially conservative, who would join coalitions with Democratic reformers.

Most of Chicago's Jewish population resides here—it is the dominant ethnic block in some wards—and the city's only genuine salt-and-pepper, house-to-house racial integration outside of Hyde Park is here. Including concentrations of blacks in the 42nd and 46th Wards, more than 55,000 blacks live in the lakefront communities, along with a slightly larger Latino population.

Everyone expected Washington to get almost all the black vote, including everything Byrne and Daley had picked up in the primary. His Task Force on Black Empowerment, led by Lu Palmer and Renault Robinson, would see to that. It was also expected that Epton would get the overwhelming majority of votes on the Southwest and Northwest sides. Latinos were expected to split, but Washington was given the edge among them. To win, he needed 15-20 percent of the white vote, a majority of the Latinos, and all the blacks.

Some lakefront independent leaders, including Alderman Martin Oberman (43rd), State Senator Dawn Clark Netsch, and State Representative Ellis Levin, had been Daley supporters in the primary. They, along with almost all the regular Democrat aldermen and legislators who had backed Byrne in the primary, quickly organized themselves into a Washington bloc. But they would complain throughout the campaign period that they could not get Washington to come into their turf nor to make the kinds of moves required to gain or hold on to the traditional lakefront reform-liberal vote.

Even the most nationalistic-minded blacks in the Washington camp understood that he needed white votes to win, and the lakefront was the most likely source. But Washington aides said privately that they had serious problems getting him to spend time in the white areas despite the recognized need. They attributed it to anxiety or quirkiness; he certainly had no problems dealing with Hyde Park whites. In the primary he had spent most of his time in his own district also, but he had required fewer white votes to win that one.

It was not until a week before the election that Washington did any serious lakefront campaigning and unveiled his 300-member transition team, an interracial group including some major business, professional, social service, and community leaders who would develop policy for the changing of the guard. This team—apart from its potential functional value for the government—was the linchpin in the white-lakefront strategy. The names were selected in part to cause reformers' juices to flow, and to demonstrate in some final way that the new administration would be competent, truly integrated, and not simply a black takeover.

The team was largely in place for more than a week before its final announcement. The press and many Washington supporters viewed the inability to get it out earlier as symptomatic of the kinds of problems the campaign was having in general, and specifically in executing its presumed white-lakefront strategy. Internal power struggles were taking their toll in confusion, and scheduling foul-ups were rife.

The *Tribune*'s political writer, David Axelrod, and the *Sun-Times*' political editor Basil Talbott each devoted several columns late in the campaign to the stuttering Washington effort, and especially the inability to broaden its base. "Washington is making Epton's negative ethnic campaign easy," wrote Talbott nine days before the election. "Washington's lethargic campaign is behaving as if it had already won."

Race, it was correctly assumed by the Epton forces, would carry their candidate only so far—but perhaps not far enough to win. There had to be some positive reasons for people to vote for Epton, and, more importantly, there had to be some reasons to vote against Washington that were unrelated to race, perhaps mainly to give voters a way to rationalize their intentions to vote racially.

It was not difficult to build a positive Epton image. He did, after all, have a fine record in the legislature; he also had a good record professionally as a lawyer and in business. Certainly good enough for a Republican. These would be embellished by a campaign biography showing him to have an undergraduate degree from the University of Chicago and a law degree from DePaul University. The biography and his radio and television commercials also said that he flew missions over Nazi Germany in World War II when he was twenty-one years old.

Only after the campaign was over did *Chicago* magazine and the *Chicago Lawyer* reveal that he in fact had no higher education degrees: he became a lawyer during the period after the war when veterans could simply pass the bar examination. The *Chicago Lawyer* also pointed out that he did not arrive in Europe until he was twenty-three, when the war was almost over.

Epton did, however, offer a stream of position papers concerned with government reform and operations. None of the points came under attack, and it is safe to say that none played any serious part in attracting or deterring voters. Similarly, the disclosure that Epton's law firm received nearly a million dollars' worth of state business did not seem to hurt him.

Epton made his real hay in a series of hard-hitting attacks on Washington's record, done in punchy broadcast commercials and reiterated endlessly in speeches and handbills. Neither Byrne nor Daley had attacked Washington in the primary, mainly out of a fear of alienating any black votes they might win. It was assumed that his federal misdemeanor conviction and bar suspension were well known and would hurt mortally. They were wrong. The Epton forces, led by John Deardourff, made no such mistake. They hammered away at the two issues and then heaped on more, beginning with the first and only televised debate of the general election on March 22. Epton produced a thick black folder and brought up not only the conviction but additional testimony made during the sentencing hearings, wherein Assistant U.S. Attorney Howard Hoffman accused Washington of not having filed returns for nineteen years—fifteen more than he had just been convicted for—and implying not only failure to file (a misdemeanor involving little more than a $500 fine) but probable tax evasion as well, a felony.

Washington tersely denied the charge, which had also come up in the 1977 race. Research by the media and by Washington himself showed nothing that could refute or support the charge, because his own records were long gone, and the Internal Revenue Service had no remaining records indicating either filing or nonfiling. Washington also made the point that if the charges were true, there was no statute of limitations preventing prosecution for those years, once the matter was in court for the four years in question.

The only person who could shed any light on the matter, Howard Hoffman, now an attorney in private practice, stayed strangely silent; he refused to comment at all on the matter, though there was no reason why he could not do so. Nevertheless, the nineteen-year allegation slipped into campaign lore through fuzzily worded "official" Epton literature and blatantly worded "unofficial" literature—along with much uglier charges of the "unofficial" brand.

The Epton black book also came up with the charge that while

Washington told the Supreme Court he had not been involved in any lawsuits during the time of his suspension, he had in fact been sued five times. The problem was, there was no way one could prove whether Washington knew about the suits, because there was no record of summonses being served. The suits themselves were minor, three of them by a landlord trying to evict him, one by the city for damages from an auto accident, and another for a housing code violation. Later, Epton would disclose that Washington had been sued several times by public utilities for unpaid debts. These turned out to be campaign-related matters, some of them settled, but all embarrassing.

Later yet, the *Sun-Times* published a story, presumably generated by Epton researchers, that Washington and two others were in arrears on property taxes on a now-abandoned slum building they owned jointly. Again, while it is difficult to prove Washington knew what was going on in the matter, it looked bad.

Emerging was a picture of a man who was exceedingly careless in handling his personal affairs and quite possibly a major deadbeat, if not a petty crook. Handled less stridently, with the kind of skill David Sawyer had demonstrated on Byrne's behalf, such attacks might have defeated Washington in the primary. They certainly were taking their toll in the general election. Every poll taken by the media and the campaigns showed a consistent attrition of white voters from Washington, especially on the north lakefront, where he had to maintain a substantial vote.

The hemorrhage of white voters might have continued to the point of final defeat had the negative impression been drilled home without the contamination of more vicious and lurid attacks through "unofficial" materials. In fact, the only poll that ever showed Washington losing was a private tracking poll by Pat Caddell on Thursday, April 7, five days before campaign's end.

Only a week earlier, a leaflet surfaced saying that the Chicago *Tribune* was suppressing an article that proved Washington had been arrested on a morals charge involving sexual misconduct with a minor. The charge, in various renditions, had been floating around for weeks. The myth was that the event had been expunged from the books but that the arresting officer or the family of the involved young man would finally come forth. No one knows how the rumor started, though one report attributed it to a Byrne policeman-bodyguard. The best investigative reporters in the city, however, could not find a shred of evidence to support any aspect of it; and, of course, the arresting officer and the family never materialized.

The leaflet urged people to call the *Tribune* and ask that the story be printed. The leaflet was traced by Hugh Hill of WLS-TV to Epton volunteer operatives working out of the 26th Ward rump organization originally set up for Jane Byrne by a Vrdolyak aide, "Tony" Rocque.

In a close judgment call, the *Tribune* decided to do a story on the leaflet, making clear that they had no such story and that they had not been able to corroborate any such story. As it turned out, the *Tribune*'s decision helped Washington, first, by beginning to clear the air of a floating rumor that was causing a lot of anxiety, and second, by demonstrating the depths to which the attacks on him had sunk, creating a counterreaction.

Washington decided to seize the issue and deal with it openly—a high-risk gambit to discredit the Epton campaign. It apparently worked: the real charges against his integrity were weakened by his exposure of the bogus one. This was one of several such high-risk moves that worked.

It is difficult to assess how much planned strategy was laid out in the Washington campaign and how much was ad hoc. There was, however, a series of strategic decisions that were enacted either by design or default that drew criticism but may collectively have helped produce the victory.

One aspect was the national Democrat strategy, which involved bringing in dozens of national figures on behalf of the candidate. In addition, it required Washington to travel to places such as Washington, D.C., New York, and Los Angeles to be feted, funded, and endorsed by their local mayors, governors, and senators. The idea was to play on the party loyalty and principles of those whites who might have serious questions about Washington either personally or racially, but who consider themselves Democrats above all else. The final results of the campaign give reason to believe that this strategy affected some whites and larger numbers of Latinos.

There was something odd, indeed, about the sight of Speaker of the House Thomas P. "Tip" O'Neill endorsing Washington from Washington and urging all good party members to go out and vote for him, while a good Chicago party member such as Dan Rostenkowski, chairman of the House Ways and Means Committee, was being evasive. People in other parts of the country did not understand that "Rusty" was a Chicago ward committeeman even before he was a highly placed congressman and that Chicago ward politics is more important to such folk than national politics. Well, all politics, they say, are local, and a lot of people in Rostenkowski's ward are not in love with people with black skins—and no Chicago ward politician is in love with reformers.

Eventually Rostenkowski endorsed Washington, though there is no evidence he turned out the troops in the candidate's behalf. But a lot of other Democrats who were not Chicago ward committeemen came in to urge a vote for Washington. Some of the choices of visiting supporters were odd—like the batch of Southern state chairmen nobody here ever heard of, and Burt Lance, whom some people heard of but hadn't heard very good things about.

Then there were presidential candidates, such as Senator Alan Cranston, the Californian who had a proprietary interest because he was the only major white Democrat on a national level to endorse Washington in the primary. Senator John Glenn of Ohio came in to give his blessing, and the Washington people decided to issue the campaign's main position papers at the same time. Typical of the frequent ineptitudes of the campaign, attention predictably was paid only to the former astronaut, while the position papers—tactically more important because they would help keep reform voters in the Democratic camp—got also-ran mention in the stories.

The Washington media strategy that went along with the visits of national figures was to play on economic fears. A clever commercial showed a limp puppet that looked much like Epton come slowly to life as the narrator told how the people pulling the strings were hardcore Republicans, such as Reagan and Governor Jim Thompson.

But the most important out-of-towner to show up, for unexpected reasons, was Walter Mondale.

The former Vice President appeared to be in a lot of trouble for backing Daley in the primary. In fact, Rev. Jesse Jackson had organized a nationwide group of black leaders to protest Mondale's action. But an endorsement of Washington in the general election might help, so the visit was set up for Palm Sunday. The candidate and the candidate were to attend services at St. Pascal's Roman Catholic Church on the far Northwest Side. Both Epton and Washington had been invited to speak at a forum there earlier in the week; neither came, but the Sunday visit looked like a good way for Washington to make points in a hostile white neighborhood.

When they arrived, they found "nigger die" spray-painted on a wall and were met by a nasty, jeering crowd of perhaps three dozen, some of whom shouted racial epithets as well as "crook," "tax cheater," and "baby killer," referring to the candidates' support of abortion. The pair entered the church, but the commotion outside was so great that they decided abruptly to leave. That event was all the national and international press needed. The television shots and still photographs went across the country and around the world, instant metaphors for what *Newsweek* headlined as "Chicago's Ugly Election" and *People* magazine bannered "Hatred Walks the Streets."

Bill Zimmerman, Harold Washington's media consultant, who would subsequently confront his counterpart Deardourff publicly for creating a racist campaign, picked up on the thing quickly. One of his commercials sensationally intercut shots of black and white children together reciting the pledge of allegiance, hands over hearts, with news footage of the heckling church crowd. A later, more daring spot began with shots from the nation's painful past two decades: the slaying of the Kennedys and Martin Luther King, the police rioting at the Democratic National Convention of 1968, and others—winding up with the jeering church mob chanting "Ep-ton-Ep-ton-Ep-ton," and asking the voters in effect not to be party to a similar scar by voting for the Republican.

This was strong medicine, aimed at a fringe of voters whose consciousness had been shaped by the events of the 1960s and early 1970s. Like the strategy of "nationalizing" the campaign, it was aimed at a small, hard core of conscience-ridden voters. Also like the nationalizing of the campaign, it opened the effort up to criticism and risked greater losses by backfiring. However, the media campaign softened the harshness of the two commercials somewhat by alternating them with a long, elegant spot that flashed images of ethnic diversity in Chicago and urged respect for the differences between peoples and unity in the election.

One can speculate on what might have happened had different approaches been taken, but the empirical proof says that all or part of the high-risk strategy worked. Lakefronters and young voters were Washington's strongest white supporters.

Epton dropped out of sight during most of the campaign's final weekend. Speculation was that the tension was getting to him, and aides figured he would pop off in some especially damaging way at the last minute. Better to lose some last-minute visibility than to lose the election because of some goof.

They were especially concerned about his regular attacks on the press—and his personal attack on *Tribune* columnist Vernon

Jarrett, a black Washington partisan. Epton refused to appear on a national telecast because of Jarrett's presence as a guest interviewer.

Epton's sudden low visibility did not go unnoticed in the press, nor was much of the speculation about its reasons muffled. After all, everyone was getting the idea that Epton was a little weird. At the Marzullo fund-raiser he had told a local TV crew it should "go back" to Russia. Weeks later, WLS-TV reporter Russ Ewing disclosed the fact that Epton had received psychiatric treatment at Michael Reese Hospital on at least two occasions. Epton said it was because of physiological problems, later diagnosed as ulcers. He said he also occasionally talked to a psychiatrist when concerned about family problems.

There was hushed speculation that Epton was not being fully candid, especially when he pointedly went against Deardourff's recommendation and refused to make his health records public. But the question of mental health did not become the major public issue the Washington forces had hoped for. On the one hand, it raised questions about Epton's stability; but on the other, the charge was viewed as out of bounds, and the issue of purloined medical records cut both ways. The episode did, however, set Epton railing against the press even more. And the more he railed. . . .

It was a peaceful election day, as election days go in Chicago. The turnout was immense: a record 82 percent of the city's 1,625,786 registered voters took ballots. That included all of the more than 45,000 people who registered to vote after the primary—a strong majority of them black. It would be a long night.

At 7:01 p.m., WLS-TV, where I was working as a political analyst for the primary and general elections, declared Washington a winner with 55 percent of the vote based on exit polls. When the news team went on the air for full-scale coverage at 9:00 p.m., they modified that number to 52 percent, based on the actual results from key precincts, only a whisker above the final official result that would be issued days later.

But the white cards were coming in first in the tabulations of the Chicago Board of Elections—and in Epton headquarters. Things were looking good for him. He came out to greet his supporters late in the evening, testily snapped at some enthusiasts whose signs were obstructing a camera's view, then announced he was very optimistic and would be back shortly.

He was not to come back.

An aide later came down to tell the crowd it was not over yet, but please to go home. There was grumbling that he was not doing right by his supporters; but then this guy was never really one of them anyway.

It all went pretty much as had been anticipated by the Washington strategists, despite the ups and downs and the scare they had from the previous Thursday's poll. Washington received almost all the black vote, carrying the nineteen predominantly black wards, the polyglot First Ward, and the Latino 22nd and 31st Wards. He even came close to carrying Marzullo's 25th! He lost Vrdolyak's 10th Ward by a two-to-one margin, the approximate ratio of whites to blacks there.

The final count was Washington 668,176, Epton 619,926. More than 42,000 people took ballots but did not vote in this mayoral election.

Epton received more than 90 percent in Pucinski's ward and did even better on the Southwest Side. His margins in the 13th and 23rd Wards exceeded 30,000 votes each. These margins were obliterated, however, by similar margins Washington ran up in the 6th, 8th, and 21st Wards of the First Congressional District. But it was the Latino and white vote along the lakefront that made the big difference—though Washington got higher than expected totals in some working-class Northwest Side wards, apparently from ethnic, die-hard Democrats who proved essential to the ultimate victory. Estimates of Washington's Latino vote ranged as high as 75 percent; his white vote was 18 percent. Though he carried no lakefront wards, his vote approached 42 percent there, except in the 50th, the most Jewish ward in the city, where he got a little more than 18 percent, just about the citywide white average.

Harold Washington beat Bernard Epton because Washington was a Democrat. The congressman's heavy, virtually unanimous black support, his strong Hispanic totals, and his respectable cut of the lakefront liberal vote might have fallen short without the hardcore backing of a measurable number of those white ethnic Democrats.

Epton carried the predominantly white ethnic wards by lopsided margins, but the 1983 Chicago mayoral battle boiled down to which candidate's area of political support would outnumber the opposition, for in this election most of the wards were won by a racial landslide. In only nine wards did the winner receive less than 60 percent of the vote, while in twenty-two of the fifty wards the victor captured 90 percent or more of the vote. Of Washington's twenty-two ward victories, he won sixteen with 90 percent or more of the vote, five with 60 percent or more, and only one with less than 60 percent. In sum, Washington's white Democratic support in Epton wards far exceeded the latter's black GOP support in Washington territory.

And yet Epton carried six more wards than did Washington, aided by the high voter turnout in the ethnic communities. A vast majority of the white ethnic Northwest and Southwest side voters supported a Republican for mayor, something that had not occurred since 1955. But it was on a much more massive scale now. Epton's best six wards, measured by both plurality and percentage of the vote (13th, 23rd, 36th, 38th, 41st, 45th), were almost entirely white and areas where Byrne and Daley had also garnered most of the primary vote. But, strong as Epton's support was in these ethnic wards, Washington had eleven wards with a higher winning percentage than Epton's best ward.

Never in Chicago's political history has a candidate swept a portion of the electorate the way Washington did the black vote. So massive was his black support that in ten black wards he received an unbelievable 99 percent of the vote, while in six other wards his percentage was over 90 percent. Black middle-class Southside wards— Washington's true home base—though unable to match the white ethnic wards in turnout, were by their large populations and near unanimity able to give the congressman margins large enough to neutralize Epton's strongholds. This factor allowed the Near Southside and Westside black wards the opportunity to use their slightly smaller Washington vote margins (percentages were similar but turnouts were smaller) to overtake Epton citywide. Thus, though Epton overall won six more wards overall than Washington did, the Democratic nominee enjoyed a two-to-one advantage in wards where he won by more than 20,000 votes.

It was a campaign cliche to say that a black candidate other than Washington might have had an easier time winning, but it is also safe to say that a white candidate other than Epton, running a less strident campaign, might have wound up mayor. Bernie Epton didn't like the fact that Washington got a big share of the Jewish vote—more than one-third, according to WMAQ-TV and the NBC exit poll. He threatened to reconsider his giving to Jewish charities, just as he had earlier threatened to reconsider his giving to black charities.

The wiseacres on the street knew all along it was going to be a tough, ethnic election.

TABLE 3

1983 Chicago Mayoral (General)

Ward	Democratic Ward Committeeman	Washington	Epton	Plurality Winner	Washington Percent	Ward Percent Voter Turnout
1	John D'Arco	13,033	7,782	5,251-W	63%	78%
2	William Barnett	22,749	558	22,191-W	98%	80%
3	Tyrone Kenner	24,472	178	24,294-W	99%	78%
4	Timothy Evans	24,428	1,984	22,444-W	93%	80%
5	Alan Dobry	24,738	2,455	22,283-W	91%	83%
6	Eugene Sawyer	35,052	240	34,812-W	99%	84%
7	Ray Castro	17,304	3,776	13,528-W	82%	78%
8	John Stroger	31,106	458	30,648-W	99%	83%
9	Robert Shaw	24,076	1,521	22,555-W	94%	83%
10	Edward Vrdolyak	10,105	19,651	9,546-E	34%	86%
11	John Daley	7,200	20,574	13,374-E	26%	86%
12	Theodore Swinarski	3,838	21,059	16,321-E	15%	84%
13	Michael Madigan	1,460	34,893	33,433-E	4%	91%
14	Edward Burke	3,864	20,117	16,253-E	16%	87%
15	Frank Savickas	15,954	10,168	5,786-W	61%	84%
16	James Taylor	25,654	221	25,433-W	99%	82%
17	Bill Parker	29,264	206	29,058-W	99%	83%
18	John Daley	14,894	19,096	4,202-E	44%	87%
19	Thomas Hynes	7,056	28,095	21,039-E	20%	85%
20	Cecil Partee	25,713	220	25,493-W	99%	79%
21	Niles Sherman	32,962	275	32,687-W	99%	85%
22	Frank Stemberk	4,674	4,279	395-W	52%	70%
23	William Lipinski	1,373	32,404	31,031-E	4%	90%
24	William Henry	24,265	129	24,136-W	99%	81%
25	Vito Marzullo	5,925	6,099	174-E	49%	73%
26	Mathew Bieszczat	7,449	8,823	1,374-E	46%	74%
27	Edward Quigley	20,710	1,577	19,133-W	93%	78%
28	William Carothers	22,339	224	22,115-W	99%	79%
29	Iola McGowan	19,884	1,531	18,353-W	93%	80%
30	Thaddeus Lechowicz	3,034	20,853	17,819-E	13%	83%
31	Edward Nedza	9,857	6,399	3,458-W	61%	75%
32	Daniel Rostenkowski	8,268	10,526	2,258-E	44%	76%
33	Richard Mell	6,909	11,298	4,389-E	38%	77%
34	Wilson Frost	29,372	336	29,036-W	99%	84%
35	John Marcin	3,414	18,661	15,247-E	16%	81%
36	William Banks	1,651	31,968	30,317-E	5%	87%
37	Frank Damato	17,555	5,254	12,301-W	77%	81%
38	Thomas Cullerton	1,883	30,942	29,059-E	6%	87%
39	Anthony Laurino	3,127	22,161	19,034-E	12%	84%
40	John Geocaris	3,772	18,217	14,455-E	17%	82%
41	Roman Pucinski	2,380	32,733	30,353-E	7%	84%
42	George Dunne	12,496	14,894	2,398-E	46%	81%
43	Daniel O'Brien	11,008	19,620	8,612-E	36%	81%
44	John Merlo	10,613	16,372	5,759-E	39%	79%
45	Thomas Lyons	2,376	31,737	29,361-E	7%	87%
46	Ralph Axelrod	10,251	11,543	1,292-E	47%	78%
47	Edmund Kelly	4,515	20,403	15,888-E	18%	81%
48	Martin Tuchow	9,433	12,269	2,836-E	44%	76%
49	Michael Brady	9,719	12,815	3,096-E	43%	77%
50	Howard Carroll	5,002	22,368	17,366-E	18%	82%
	WARDS WON:	22	28			
	TOTAL:	668,176	619,926	48,250-W	51.8%	82%

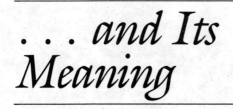

. . . and Its Meaning

VII

Observations and Reflections on the Current and Future Directions of the Chicago Democratic Machine

MILTON RAKOVE

"In the 1983 mayoral primary the machine lost control of the black vote, and in the general election the machine lost control of the white vote. So the machine has lost absolute control of both the white and the black vote in Chicago. And, of course, what has happened now is not only that race has replaced ethnicity in the city, but race has replaced party identification in the city. People don't identify as Democrats or Republicans very much any more. They identify now as blacks or whites in Chicago."

—Milton Rakove

What is the Chicago Democratic machine? Where has it been, where is it now, and where is it going? A lot of people call it the Richard J. Daley Machine, but the machine was there a quarter of a century before Daley, and he had it for almost another quarter of a century. Thus, the machine has been in business now for about fifty years. It started in 1931 when Chicago's mayor, Anton Cermak, and his two leading advisers, Patrick Nash and Edward Kelly, put it together. Former Mayor Jane Byrne, in one of the recent mayoral primary debates, said that the 11th Ward had been controlling the city for 100 years. Well, she made Paris 4,000 years old instead of 1,000, so those numbers don't mean anything.

If you understand the machine, you understand that it's more than a political organization. It's a composite thing that traditionally has been made up of essentially three elements in the community. First, there is the political organization, the ward committeemen, the precinct workers, or what they call in City Hall the "precint" workers, in the organization. That's one part of the machine. The second integral part of the machine is the city and county govern-

127

ment, which has been intimately tied into the machine in a relationship somewhat analogous to the one in Russia between the Communist party and Soviet government. For many Chicagoans, the party is more important than the government itself. And third, of course, it is made up of the powerful private groups in the community itself—the businessmen, the labor unions, and the bankers; but it also reaches into ethnic groups, the Catholic Church, and the North Michigan Avenue Association, three constituent elements.

The machine has operated traditionally on the basis of three basic guiding principles: first, the concept of loyalty; second, the concept of efficiency; and third, the concept of adaptability. What does that mean? Well, if you were a part of that machine, if you were a worker or part of the city government, or a banker or a businessman or leader of a labor union, you would be required to give your primary loyalty to the interests of the machine. The machine has always allowed people in it who have subsidiary loyalties. You can look out for your own interests up to a point; but if there is a conflict between your interests and the interests of the machine, the machine comes first and your interests come second. I remember a Southwest Side alderman told me that when they introduced the first Open Occupancy Bill in the City Council, Daley called him and said, "I need your vote." The alderman said, "I can't do that because if I vote that way, my family will have to move out of the neighborhood." And Daley said, "Well, what's more important, your family or the party? Now make a choice right here." If you were Catholic, Daley didn't mind if you paid your loyalty to the church; but if it was a choice between what he needed and what the Pope needed, you had better side with Daley, because the Pope might get you later but Daley would get you now. If they asked you to run, you ran. If they told you not to run, you did not run. You waited your turn. That's what it used to be like.

Some may know the story of "Bicycle Jim" Bowler, who was an old Irish alderman/committeeman in the 25th Ward for forty years preceding Vito Marzullo. That ward has had only three aldermen and committeemen in this century: Bowler, Vito Marzullo, and the infamous Johnny Powers, the lifelong nemesis of Jane Addams. Bowler was the alderman and committeeman for many years, and he wanted to be a congressman. But the incumbent congressman was A. J. Sabbath, who was a Bohemian Jew and a powerful committeeman from the 21st Ward. Bowler could not go to Congress until Sabbath died. Sabbath finally died at the age of eighty, giving Bowler the opportunity to become a frisky seventy-eight-year-old freshman congressman. One day Sam Rayburn, the Speaker of the House, said to Bowler: "Why did they send you here at such an age? Why did you come?" Bowler said simply, "It was my turn." So you gave your loyalty first to the machine.

Secondly, the machine insisted on efficiency. You had a piece of the action, and you had to take care of it. You had a ward, you delivered that ward; you had a precinct, you delivered that precinct. You ran a department, you took care of that department, and never mind what was going on anywhere else. Don't ask yourself what's going on in the next precinct; that was not your business. What was going on in the city or in the other wards should not concern you. If you did not deliver your ward and the machine won an election, Daley would have you down there the next day; and instead of saying, "We won," Daley would say, "You lost." One of the great strengths of the machine throughout its history was its decentralization of political responsibility combined with its centralization of political authority.

Now the third thing about the machine was its adaptability. The machine has demonstrated an amazing ability through most of its history to adapt to a changing city environment. The machine was built originally on the ethnic principle. At the outset the Irish ran the show, keeping the good things for themselves and giving out whatever was left to the other ethnic groups in the city on the basis of their contribution to the machine. For example, the Irish got the mayor, county board chairman, chairman of the party, state's attorney, county clerk, superintendent of police, fire superintendent, president of the board of education; the Poles got county treasurer, the Jews got city treasurer, the Bohemians got city clerk, and the Scandinavians got county recorder of deeds.

As the city changed, the machine changed. It shifted its power base from the ethnic wards to the black wards. As blacks came into the city in large numbers, the white ethnics began moving out of Chicago—or at least out to the fringe areas of the city—and their contribution to the machine diminished. So for a long time the machine insisted on loyalty and efficiency, and it practiced adaptability.

The machine and its politicians also had three major objectives. One was getting into office; the second was staying there as long as possible; and the third was getting as much out of it as one could. How do you get into office? Well, Daley used to say you get into office by getting more votes than the other guy. When traditional machine politicians ran for office they appealed to people's basic instincts—their private interests. They did not appeal to public interests. The old adage was that you appeal to voters' private interests, pacify those concerns, and then say this is good for the public interest. So you ran for office trying to get votes and talking about what you would do for people.

How do you stay in office? Well, the machine has always operated on the principle that the best way to stay in office is to do nothing. Political scientists have never understood the machine political strategy of running for office saying you can do something, and then when you get in, doing nothing. Why do you do nothing? Well, because every time you do something, somebody gets angry. So if you do nothing, nobody gets angry. It's very hard for people to get mad if you do nothing. Every time you make a political decision, somebody wins and somebody loses. And, of course, the ones who won—you don't get them because they're ungrateful. They forget what you did for them—*immediately*. Say you did something for someone in the precinct. The precinct captain would go around and phone some voter who hadn't shown up yet and say, "You haven't voted yet." And the voter says, "It's cold outside." The precinct captain says, "Remember what I did for you six months ago?" And the voter says, "What have you done for me lately?" They're ungrateful. But the ones you did something *to,* you don't have to get them out. Fifteen degrees below, ten feet of snow, and they're mushing down to the polling places at 5:30 in the morning to pull that lever to get you. So the best thing to do is nothing. And if you have to do anything, you do as little as you can about as much as possible.

How do you reap the rewards of office? Well, the rewards of office are basically three things for politicians: jobs, money, and status. And the machine, of course, had the ability to hand those kinds of things out. Jobs, money, and status translated into power, wealth, and influence.

Now let me turn to the other things the machine did in Chicago for a long time throughout its history. It had several functions. One of its primary functions was to choke off reform in the city. The machine resisted reform because reform was bad for the machine. However, the machine was also throughout its history something of an avenue by which people could get into the action somehow, get a piece of the pie—political, economic, social, and so forth. You could do a lot of that through the machine. It was a device through which many people who otherwise could not make it would get into the action. The machine has also been throughout most of its history an ongoing, stabilizing institution in the city that dampened violent change. Significant change in the city had to come through the machine, and the machine was very resistant to that kind of thing. So the machine was a kind of mixed blessing. It wasn't just a curse on Chicago: it provided some means for people to get ahead in the city, but it also blocked reform.

The machine has been in three periods so far: the pre-Daley era, the Daley era, and what we're in now—the post-Daley era. In each of these periods the power base of the machine shifted from time to time. Before Daley, the party—the political organization— was the most important part of the machine. The ward committee- men ran the city. Former alderman Tom Keane told me a few years ago that in the old days the budget was made up by eight or ten powerful ward committeemen who were also aldermen. They passed out the goodies. The city government was controlled by the party organization—again, somewhat analogous to what it is like in Rus- sia, where the Communist party is more important than the Soviet government. The committeemen controlled the City Council, they controlled the bureaucracy; and the powerful, private interest groups usually had to go to politicians to get things done.

Now, that changed when Daley came in. Daley took the city government away from the ward committeemen. The power base shifted from the machine, from the political organization, to Daley himself. Daley became the central focus of the machine. A few years ago I interviewed former alderman and mayoral candidate Bill Singer, and we talked about the Council and when Bill was an alderman. He said that Daley ran the Council, that the Council was not re- sponsible to the machine but to Daley. Daley got control of the budget, which gave him control of jobs and money, which are the two things that really count in the machine. He also took over control of the bureaucracy, and he passed out the rewards. He be- came so powerful that he decided who would run for every office. He controlled the county because he picked the county officehold- ers; he controlled the city delegations to Springfield; and he con- trolled the Democratic delegations to Congress. So Daley was more than a mayor and a party chairman. He had a great deal of power because his control reached beyond the city into the county and down to the legislature in Springfield, and out to Washington, D.C. Daley changed the power structure within the machine by person- alizing its power under his authority.

Now, what happened after Daley died? The power structure of the machine began to shift even farther away from the ward committeemen to the mayor and the bureaucracy. Mayor Michael Bilandic and Mayor Jane Byrne both had control of the bureaucracy, and they had control of the jobs. And that gave them control of the Council. The way the Council behaved in the post-Daley years was as if Daley were still alive. They followed Mayor Bilandic and Mayor Byrne as if Daley were still mayor. The only difference was that neither Bilandic nor Byrne was Daley. Bilandic did not have Daley's charismatic ability, and he didn't control the whole scene the way Daley did. And, of course, neither did Mayor Byrne. Mayor Byrne didn't have Daley's ability, she didn't have his kind of power, she didn't have his grasp of finance, and she didn't have his background in the bureaucracy. In short, she could not fill his shoes.

THE CONTEMPORARY SITUATION

In 1926, H. L. Mencken described how he thought democracy worked in his book called—appropriately enough—*Notes on Democracy*. According to Mencken,

> The truth is that in a democracy the sovereign mob must employ agents to execute its will, but the agents may have ideas of their own based on interests of their own and the means at hand to do and get what they will. Moreover, their very position gives them the power of influencing the electors that is far above that of any ordinary citizen. They become politicians ex officio and usually end up by selling such influence as remains after they've taken all they need for their own end. The great masses of Americans look for leading to professional politicians who are influenced in turn by small but competent and determined minorities with special knowledge and special interests. They are thus constantly bamboozled and exploited by small minorities of their own number, by determined and ambitious individuals, and even by exterior groups. But all the while they have the means in their hands to halt the obscenity whenever it becomes intolerable and now and then rise transiently to a sort of intelligence and they do put a stop to it.

What Mencken is saying is basically what goes on. You've got the people out there who have the power, and ostensibly they exercise the power; but what they do is choose agents who *actually* exercise the power. And, of course, what the agents do is, first, represent themselves and their own interests, and second, represent the powerful private interests, and last, represent the needs of the people out there. And that's why Mencken says that every once in a while the people rise up and put a halt to that obscenity and throw the rogues out of office.

I think that is basically what happened in Chicago in 1983. A substantial part of the population has risen up to throw the rogues out of office and to create a new situation in Chicago. Now you could see that situation building over the past few years. You could see that the machine was weakening and that something was happening in Chicago that sooner or later would cause an explosion in the city. Daley's great strength as mayor, more than anything, was the fact that he was a master power broker. He understood power and how to use it. And essentially, Daley understood and practiced interest group politics. He would give every powerful interest group some of the action in the city. In return, that powerful interest group then had to support Daley and what Daley conceived to be the public interest of the city.

Now the public interest, as he conceived it, didn't always coincide with what a number of people thought the public interest should be. However, Daley was a man who was truly concerned about the public interest as he saw it, and he practiced this kind of private interest group politics and brokered power to try to make Chicago into what he thought was a great city. He would give the bankers what they wanted; they in turn would support him. He would give the State Street Council what they wanted, and they would support him. He would give the labor unions what they wanted—the prevailing wage rate and things like that—and they would support him. He would give the ward committeemen what they wanted and needed: jobs for their wards, things for themselves, and good public services. In return, he expected them to support him on whatever he wanted for the city.

As political power shifted in the city, so did the manner in which Daley responded to political demands. When Daley came into office, the city machine practiced white ethnic politics. But as Daley's term in office advanced, the blacks became a very substantial, much more important component of the city body politic. What Daley had to do then was balance off ethnic politics with racial politics. The white ethnics united as a white bloc, and the blacks became a strong bloc, and race transcended ethnicity as the bottom line in Chicago politics.

Daley gave the blacks what he thought they wanted and needed: jobs, welfare, and public services. And he gave the whites what he thought they needed and wanted: segregation. And if he gave the whites segregation, they didn't care if he gave the blacks jobs, welfare, and public services. If he gave the blacks jobs, welfare, and public services, they didn't care a great deal about whether he integrated the city. This arrangement began to come apart only in Daley's last years in office.

Precipitating this political change in Chicago was the rise to power of a very substantial black middle class that no longer wanted jobs, welfare, and public services; they wanted real political power. They wanted a chance to be mayor, and the white ethnics were unwilling to give that up. The machine couldn't come to terms with or resolve this new political challenge. Throughout the 1970s one could see the change building out in the black community. In 1972 former Cook County State's Attorney Edward Hanrahan's re-election bid was quashed by a black revolt against his candidacy. Four years later, Daley's hand-picked congressional candidate Erwin France was unable to defeat incumbent Congressman Ralph Metcalfe in a hotly contested First District primary. The city council and the state legislature saw independent blacks elected to office; and finally in 1979, blacks gave the Democratic mayoral challenger Jane Byrne an upset primary victory over machine incumbent Michael Bilandic. In 1983 the rising tide of black independence made Congressman Harold Washington the city's first black mayor.

The black political movement in Chicago in 1983 was uncontrolled by the machine. I think essentially what happened in Chicago and possibly other Northern cities may be the second half of the great civil rights drive. What Martin Luther King started in the South in the 1960s may now be happening in the North. And Chicago may be the kickoff for a new black political awakening. Many will remember when King came to Chicago in 1966 to integrate the city. He said that blacks were the balance of power in the city. Daley defeated King in that confrontation: King went home with nothing for his efforts. It was premature, it was too early; but now it has come to fruition in Chicago. The powerful black middle class is no longer under the control of the machine. In the 1983 mayoral primary the machine lost control of the black vote, and in the general election the machine lost control of the white vote. So the machine has lost absolute control of both the white and the black vote in Chicago. And, of course, what has happened now is not only that race has replaced ethnicity in the city, but race has replaced party identification in the city. People don't identify as Democrats or Republicans very much any more. They identify now as blacks or whites in Chicago.

Now this comes up against the traditional practices of politicians. I think you have two separate forces at work: you have the traditional practices of politicians who want to get into office and stay there as long as possible and pass out the rewards of office, primarily to themselves; on the other hand, you have an uncontrollable electorate out there that has become very difficult to deal with. In this situation Chicago politicians instinctively resort to the survival strategy of doing nothing. "Don't make no waves." And if you have to do something, do as little as possible about as much as you can in this kind of situation. Thus you have the traditional political struggle for power now counterbalanced by what is clearly a simmering race issue in the city, which manifested itself in the primary and the general election and now is boiling over in the city council. How are they doing?

Well, the blacks won the first battle: they won the mayoralty, but not the war. The whites have tentatively won the second battle— the battle in the City Council—but they have not won the war either. And the politicians on both sides, black and white, know that the real problem is not each other; the problem is the people out there. That's the real enemy out there, because an aroused public is dangerous for any politician, black or white, Republican or Democrat. Politicians don't know what voters are going to do when they get angry. Whom do they get angry at? Anybody in office. Chicago pols have a real problem in trying to deal with this movement. Political warfare in the City Council may now well spill over into all kinds of other things. It may spill over into upcoming Democratic party organization contests; it may spill over into the county; it may spill over into Springfield legislative matters; and it could spill over into Congress, this black-white confrontation.

For example, in 1984 Chicagoans will elect Democratic and Republican ward committeemen (the latter committeemen matter little in city politics). There are sixteen black Democratic ward committeemen and thirty-four white ward committeemen in the city. My own guess as to what's going to happen is that the black ward committeemen who supported Jane Byrne and opposed Harold Washington in the mayoral primary are in trouble. Several have visibly made peace with the new mayor, but those who saw their wards elect pro-Washington aldermen in 1983 will be facing a ward committeeman challenge in 1984. Every politician I ever met, as soon as he gets elected to something, starts thinking about what's next. If you're an alderman, can you be a state representative? If you're a representative, can you be a state senator? A state senator can be a U.S. congressman, and a U.S. congressman can be a Senator, and a Senator can be President or Vice President. But in Chicago politics, being a ward committeeman was the ultimate political office you could hold.

In the old days in Chicago the above process worked in reverse as well. You went to Daley and asked, "What else have you got?" Suppose you were a congressman for fourteen years and got to be chairman of an important subcommittee; and then you ran against Charles Percy for the Senate and you lost by a million votes. You went to see Daley and said, "What now?" And Daley would say, "How would you like to be alderman?" This was the real-life political scenario of Roman Pucinski in 1972: Pucinski told Daley, "I'll take it." Back in 1976, when Daley died, Jesse Jackson told Alderman Wilson Frost that he should be the acting mayor. Frost thought he *was* council mayor pro tem, and so he went up to the fifth floor of City Hall; but those Irish pols locked the door so he couldn't get in. And when Frost realized that he didn't have the numbers, he said, "What else have you got?" And they said, "How would you like to be finance committee chairman?" And Frost said, "I'll take it."

So what else is around? politicians are asking today, and where can they go from here? I would guess that those black aldermen are thinking about being ward committeemen now. And what you may get then is a very deep split in the party. It's not just those sixteen black wards. There are two wards—the 15th and the 37th—that are 60 percent black and have two white committeemen. And then you've got a couple of wards, like the 1st and the 18th, that are getting close to 50 percent black. One can well imagine that 1st Ward Committeeman John D'Arco may have a challenge. What happened to poor D'Arco in the recent ward reapportionment? They took nine of 25th Ward Committeeman Vito Marzullo's best black precincts and gave them to D'Arco. D'Arco thought he was getting a good thing, but these nine black precincts went for Washington and may well vote against him for committeeman. As for Marzullo, he has all those revolutionary Mexicans, and they're getting ready to try to throw him out if he doesn't quit himself.

What does all this mean for Chicago's future? It could mean, in a sense, a semiparalyzed government in which nothing gets done, or very little gets done. Certain things will, of course, get done: they have to pick up the garbage and get the snow off the streets, and the police have to arrest the criminals, and the firemen have to chase the fires. Those kinds of things will get done. But when you want to formulate public policies and move in new directions, how do you do that? Unless you can arrive at some agreement between the people on both sides who are willing to make a deal, you have a problem. In this current situation there are two problems: 1) can the politicians make a deal? and 2) if they can make a deal, can they enforce the deal with their constituents? Nobody knows, least of all the politicians. So we may have a period of three or four years in which there is a stalemate in the city government.

What does all this mean in terms of the machine itself? It means that the old machine that was created back in the 1930s and which Daley governed for a quarter of a century is on the critical list. I'm not sure if it will die, but even if this machine comes to an end, machine politics may rise again in Chicago. And one thing is for sure: politics is not going to be dead. Politics is going to be practiced by somebody. The question is, who is going to practice the politics over the next few years in Chicago, and what organizational direction will this politics take?

EPILOGUE*

Politics is the lifeblood of Chicago. It is the vital fluid that gives the city its energy and direction. Thus to most Chicagoans the political melee following Washington's mayoral victory was not unexpected or surprising.

The logic for such a battle went as follows. The regular Democratic organization led by Cook County Chairman Alderman Edward Vrdolyak had lost a crucial mayoral primary. In the subsequent general election most white Democratic ward committeemen either gave their party's nominee (Washington) little help or openly supported his Republican opponent, Bernard Epton. Both elections were major defeats for the machine. However, most politically street-smart Chicagoans believed the organization that had ruled the city for over a half century was not going to roll over and meekly surrender its power to the new mayor.

At first some organization operatives thought that they could work out a political accommodation with Washington. Four years earlier, the machine had lost a bitter mayoral primary to an upstart, reform-minded candidate, Jane Byrne, but had quickly made peace with her and cut a deal to run the city. However, in April 1983 attempts at accommodation and compromise were frustrated not only by the inability of the leaders to work out a suitable arrange-

*This addendum was written by Paul M. Green.

ment but also by the very forces that had propelled the new mayor into office—the black political movement.

Washington was in a tough spot following his April 12 victory. By nature, he is a careful and cautious politician, but the political euphoria in the black community was beyond his control. Candidate Washington had promised change for Chicago. He had predicted a new day for the city and its citizens—especially black Chicagoans. Several Washington boosters had gone to City Hall the day after the election and for hours rode the elevators, walked into offices, and generally basked in the victory of not just a man but a people. Knowledgeable black politicians called the triumph "a miracle from God" and spoke of the moral uplift in every ghetto neighborhood in the city.

Facing this array of hopes and expectations the new mayor was not a "free agent" to wheel and deal in traditional political terms. His supporters wanted instant tribute—immediate gratification and undeniable recognition of this newly won power. As a result, the mayor and his aides were unable to use the force of their office to piece together a working city council majority.

Moreover, it is by no means certain that even a politically free Washington could have found a mechanism to win over a council majority. Race had given his Republican opponent, Epton, more votes in one election than the combined total of the previous three GOP mayoral challengers. Racial politics had supplanted ethnic politics in Chicago and any Northwest or Southwest Side alderman who sided with Washington was courting political annihilation. None did.

Old political feuds were ended, glossed over, or put on the back burner as ethnic politicians circled their collective political wagons. Byrne and State's Attorney Richard M. Daley supporters, who weeks before were fighting each other with fanatical fury, were now allies united by a common desire—political survival. Many of these pols still despised each other, but recent primary wounds and conflicting ambitions were put aside as Washington made clear his intentions to change Chicago's power structure. He called it reform—they called it a black takeover.

The unification of white ethnic Democratic organization council members still might not have been realized without the untiring efforts of 10th Ward Alderman and Democratic County Chairman Edward Vrdolyak. Overlooked in the excitement and drama of the two 1983 mayoral contests was the elevation of Vrdolyak as Chicago's unquestioned ethnic leader. Washington's two victories had given the 10th Ward alderman something he could not achieve by him-self—the elimination of Jane Byrne as a potential rival leader and the demotion of Richard M. Daley as the other main alternative. Thus, the election of Chicago's first black mayor was a political windfall for the man who emerged as the new mayor's chief antag-onist—Edward Vrdolyak.

Living up to his nickname "Fast Eddie," Vrdolyak by political hard work and hard talk pieced together a working majority of twenty-nine aldermen in the council. His twenty-nine included the council's only Hispanic member. Washington was left with the coun-cil's sixteen black aldermen plus five white independent aldermen along the lakefront. The battle lines were drawn, and the combatants quickly became known as the Vrdolyak 29 and the Washington 21.

Without question, race was the key to this council confron-tation. Many black aldermen were longtime Democratic organiza-tion stalwarts and close associates of Vrdolyak. Like their white ethnic colleagues they too had no choice but to vote with their color. As with the Vrdolyak 29, the Washington 21 was made up of indi-viduals who in the past were openly hostile to their new leader. However, the racial pressure was too strong for any of them to cut a deal outside of their own color lines.

The Vrdolyak 29-Washington 21 mentality transcended the council and moved on to all other aspects of city life. Whatever the rhetoric, the main battle prize was power. As Milton Rakove said, "Politics is going to be practiced by somebody. The question is who's going to practice the politics over the next few years in Chi-cago and what organizational direction will this politics take." In-deed, Rakove's prophecy was being played out as the once unified Chicago Democratic machine sped out of control heading for what seemed almost certain destruction. The battle lines hardened with each passing political test of strength; the moderates lost influence and significance as more explicitly racial leaders emerged.

One year into the Washington administration it seems certain that the Mayor and Vrdolyak are headed for a titanic struggle in 1987 (the next mayoral election). Discipline on both sides seems solid, and one is hard-pressed to conjure up a scenario that would shake either leader's support. Also looming on the horizon is the potential rebirth of the Chicago Republican party. The GOP, long a political doormat in the city, has hinted that it wants to create an ethnically based party structure geared to capturing traditional Dem-ocratic voters in white neighborhoods. To that end Republican leaders have slated former Chicago Police Superintendent Richard Brezczek to run for Cook County state's attorney in 1984.

Perhaps it was inevitable that middle-class blacks would revolt against the white leadership of a party and a city that they believed did not give them a fair share of the power. Nevertheless the tenacity by which the old guard wants to hold on and the high risks that each side is willing to take simply reinforces Mr. Dooley's old truism about Chicago politics: "It ain't bean bag."

VIII

Is Chicago Ready for Reform?—or,
A New Agenda for Harold Washington

WILLIAM J. GRIMSHAW

"Chicago is even less ready for reform now than it was when Bauler
supplied his triumphant shout for the history books some thirty years
ago. The classic urban reform movement, which played such a sig-
nificant role in shaping big-city politics, is a phenomenon whose
time has come and gone."

—William J. Grimshaw

INTRODUCTION

Is Chicago ready for reform? On the eve of Richard J. Daley's first
mayoral term in 1955, that remarkable philosopher-king from the old
43rd Ward, Alderman Mathias "Paddy" Bauler, triumphantly shouted,
"Chicago ain't ready for reform." Yet, despite the firmness with
which Bauler made his assertion, he really did not have all the evidence going his way. After all, Robert Merriam, Daley's reform-
minded opponent that year, had carried twenty-one of the city's fifty
wards and picked up 45 percent of the vote. Also, when Daley's
reform-oriented predecessor, Martin Kennelly, won in 1947, he recorded the largest mayoral vote ever in Chicago—before or since.
Chicago clearly had, then, a substantial number of reform-minded
voters.

 Yet while the empirical basis for "Paddy" Bauler's claim was
shaky, there is no denying the accuracy of his gut political instincts.
His man Richard Daley, despite some confusion over his goals at
the outset, turned out to be no reformer by any stretch of the imag-
ination, and Daley was very successful at the polls. Daley expanded
his electoral base over the years—save toward the end, when his
black support fell off sharply—to the point where reform was virtually eliminated as an issue in Chicago's politics.

So it is difficult to disagree with Paddy Bauler. Indeed, I am not only going to agree with Paddy, I will go him one better. Chicago is even less ready for reform now than it was when Bauler supplied his triumphant shout for the history books some thirty years ago. The classic urban reform movement, which played such a significant role in shaping big-city politics, is a phenomenon whose time has come and gone. The middle class, which spearheaded and supported the classic urban reform movement, has by and large deserted the city. When the middle class left the big cities for the suburbs, reform became a dead issue. The argument is straightforward enough to be put in syllogistic terms:

Reform is a style of politics supported by the middle class.
Chicago has lost much of its middle class since the 1950s.
Therefore, there is now little support for reform in Chicago.[1]

The argument rests upon the close relationship that exists between social structure and political style. The psychologist Sigmund Freud once observed that "anatomy is destiny." In a similar oversimplified way, it may be said that social structure determines political destiny. The Daley machine is often credited with eliminating reform. However, the decline of reform during Daley's term coincided closely with the middle-class flight to the suburbs, which began in earnest during the 1950s. As Chicago increasingly became a "warehouse for the poor," support for reform no longer could be found, except in odd pockets such as Hyde Park and the environs of the Chicago Historical Society on the near North Side. Thus, the Daley machine was a prime beneficiary of white flight.

Harold Washington's Triumph

Having stipulated with this argument the conventional wisdom about the decline of reform politics, how does one analyze Chicago's recent mayoral election? Harold Washington, Chicago's new mayor, is a reformer. His election constitutes a remarkable contradiction because it runs directly counter to the conventional wisdom concerning the relationship between social structure and political style.

Harold Washington should not have won. To begin with, there is simply not enough of a middle class left in Chicago to successfully sustain a reform-oriented mayoral candidate. Compounding the problem, Washington should not have received many black votes. Blacks disproportionately occupy the low rungs of the socioeconomic ladder, and so they should have been the least inclined to support a reform candidate. Yet black voters turned out in record numbers, and they gave Congressman Washington an extraordinary

The late, great Mayor Richard J. Daley, 1955-1976, the last of the big-time bosses who brought the Chicago political machine to such a peak of efficiency that it had no rival in all of Chicago's history. *(Holime)*

During the primary Richard M. Daley eagerly sought votes in the city's liberal lakefront wards. At an Ash Wednesday Belmont Hotel rally, Daley is joined by State Senator Dawn Clark Netsch, County Board President George Dunne, and 43rd Ward Alderman Martin Oberman. *(Chicago Sun-Times)*

Republican candidate Bernard E. Epton was all but ignored during the primary campaigns because the media found the questions of race, gender, and dynasty in the Democratic party more newsworthy. Here candidate Epton emerges briefly from his nonpersonhood for media attention on Chicago's Channel 7. *(WLS-TV/Chicago; Lauren Shay)*

Modern pollsters such as Richard Day (center) tracked public opinion throughout the campaign, while political pundits such as Hugh Hill (left) of WLS-TV and Don Rose (right) translated statistical findings that showed Mayor Jane Byrne's strength waning as the primary election approached. *(WLS-TV)*

Traditionally all Chicagoans and especially the politicians have a bit of Irish in them on St. Patrick's Day. In 1983 Mayor Jane Byrne hoped the parade would ignite support for her sudden and ill-fated reentry into the mayoral race as a write-in candidate. *(Chicago* Sun-Times*)*

A glum-faced Mayor Jane Byrne presiding over the dying days of a one-term administration, 1979—1983. The agony of defeat is not pleasant to experience, for as Jane Byrne reminisced, "I went to the polling place sixteen points ahead and ended up three points behind. . . . I felt like a member of the family had died." *(Office of the Mayor)*

Mayoral candidates Harold Washington and Bernard Epton appear very serious in their one and only face-to-face debate.

(Chicago Sun-Times; *John H. White)*

A rare photo of Epton and Washington campaign posters side by side on a South Side street corner. Most neighborhoods featured either one or the other depending upon the ethnic composition of the community. *(Chicago* Sun-Times*)*

Getting out the vote on election day, Donald Catton, a Washington aide, is seen here with a bullhorn in hand, urging South Side residents to "Punch 8 — Don't Be Late — Don't Hesitate." *(Chicago* Sun-Times*)*

The day after at a post-election "unity" breakfast, Mayor-elect Harold Washington dines with his vanquished foes. On the far left is Judge Saul Epton who substituted for his brother, defeated Republican candidate Bernard E. Epton. *(Chicago Sun-Times)*

Healing the wounds in a very Catholic city, here mayoral winner Harold Washington visits with Chicago's prince of the church, Joseph Cardinal Bernardin. *(Al Cato)*

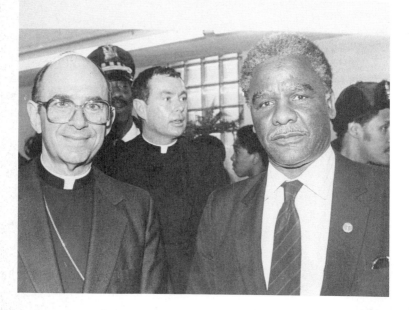

Chicago is a city of neighborhoods where ethnocultural concerns run high at any change in political landscape. Harold Washington was severely criticized during the campaign for not campaigning among whites until the end of the election. Here he is seen in a post-election visit to one of the areas where he faced opposition, Chicago's Northwest Side. *(City of Chicago)*

Mayor Harold Washington shaking hands with 10th Ward Alderman and Democratic County Chairman Edward Vrdolyak before the fateful first city council session at which Vrdolyak took over the meeting after Washington adjourned it and left the hall. This fracas set up the ongoing aldermanic battle between the "Vrdolyak 29" and the "Washington 21."

(Chicago Sun-Times*)*

Mathias "Paddy" Bauler, a North Side saloonkeeper and thirty-year veteran of the Chicago city council, appears here with his beery smile and silk top hat. Bauler was famous for his saying "Chicago ain't ready for reform yet." Even though the election battle of 1983 is over, there is no substantial evidence to contradict Paddy's prophecy. *(Holime)*

level of support. In the lower-income black ward that I managed for Harold Washington on election day, he received over 94 percent of the vote, with an unprecedented turnout of nearly 80 percent. He did even better in the middle-income black wards.

What happened? Proponents of the conventional wisdom would point out that the development is not nearly so puzzling as I am making it out to be. A combination of racial pride and substantial discounting of campaign rhetoric turned the trick for Harold Washington in the black wards. Emotionally charged by the prospect of electing one of their own, black voters simply ignored Washington's reformist campaign rhetoric and voted for the man. According to the conventional wisdom, then, Washington won in spite of, rather than because of, his reform platform.

This interpretation has an interesting corollary. Once the emotional high of the victory wears off, large numbers of black voters will once again be confronted by the grim reality of their harsh circumstances. As the reality sinks in, they will begin to demand that their reform-minded mayor begin acting like a machine-style boss. "To the victor belongs the spoils" is the style of politics that lower-income blacks need, understand, and prefer. Thus the only significant difference in Washington's victory is that blacks will displace the Irish in the city's political pecking order.

This is a seductive interpretation. It is altogether consistent with what we know about the relationship between poor voters and machine politics. The poor represent the very backbone of the political machine's support. Nevertheless, I want to present an alternative to the conventional wisdom. I believe that a cultural component needs to be added to the strictly social-class argument that has been put forth. The political experience of black citizens— in the long term as well as the short term—has provided them with a basic political value orientation that differs significantly from what tends to be held by white citizens.

Here is the problem with the conventional wisdom as I see it. It errs by presenting a false dichotomy. Political preference is limited to a choice between the machine style and the reform style of government. I believe, however, that blacks may well be articulating a preference for a third alternative style of government.

Machine politics revolves around power. Benefits are distributed to those who are deemed worthy by the machine, and they are withheld from the unworthy—those who have voted "wrong." Machine politics amounts to an exchange relationship: benefits for votes. The model for machine politics is the club: those in the club benefit, while those who are not, lose out. Reform politics, on the other hand, revolves around efficiency. The goal here is not to reward friends and punish enemies; rather, it is to attain high cost-benefit ratios. Benefits are dispensed, then, in the most rational, cost-effective manner. The model for reform politics is the business corporation. The third alternative, which is being expressed by blacks, revolves around neither power nor efficiency. *The objective is fairness.*[2] Thus, equity displaces power and efficiency as the basic principle of distribution. The model for the new black politics is the church.

Since the three alternatives are models, or ideal types, pure cases of the three are obviously not going to show up in actual practice. But one of the three basic value orientations will be given greater weight in the policy-making process. Substantial differences will turn up in the issues of to whom, on what basis, and at what cost city services are provided. To cast the distinction in the starkest terms, it makes a significant difference whether policy decisions are made chiefly on the basis of political (power), economic (efficiency), or moral (fairness) terms. My basic proposition is that blacks are more likely than whites to opt for the moral principle of distribution.

The difference stems from the different political experience of blacks and whites. Big-city politics has historically been a form of social class warfare among whites. Lower-income whites, who backed the machine, contested middle- and upper-income whites, who advanced the cause of reform. Even in Chicago—although reform has been less successful here—social class conflict has been the best general explanation of the city's politics until quite recently.[3]

Blacks were only marginal actors in this historical conflict that shaped the basic structure of big-city politics. To begin with, blacks in large numbers came to the North late, and the machine-reform conflict die had already been cast when they arrived. When the Democratic machine established its hegemony over Chicago's politics at the outset of the 1930s, blacks constituted only about 7 percent of the city's population; during the Great Depression their number increased modestly, so that by 1940 the black population made up slightly more than 8 percent of the city's population. Moreover, the Democratic machine was established with scant assistance from Chicago's black voters. A majority of black voters resisted the appeals of the machine for a remarkably long period of time. Well after the Republican party had gone out of business as a city organization, large numbers of blacks persisted in their Republican orientation. One of the city's three black aldermen was a Republican as late as

1954. Up until the mid-fifties the black wards cast their ballots evenly between the machine and Republican mayoral nominees.[4]

Finally, even after black voters had entered into the local Democratic fold and become a critical part of the machine's electoral support, few benefits were distributed to the black ward organizations, and the black community as a whole profited even less. Blacks continued to experience discrimination right across the board: in employment, housing, schooling, health care, and on down to recreation.[5] Mayor Daley used a divide-and-conquer strategy: he pitted the black ward leaders against one another, which left them unwilling and unable to take any united action on their constituents' or even their own behalf.

It can be said, then, that blacks have had less experience with machine politics, they came around slowly and late in support of the machine, and when they did give the machine their support, few rewards were forthcoming. As for the other great white political game, the reform movement, it remained mainly the province of the professional and managerial class. Since the vast majority of blacks were employed in lower occupational positions, few of them perceived reform politics to be geared to their interests.

So we may conclude that the machine was primarily the value-nurturing institution of lower-income whites. They were the ones who supported the machine over the long haul, and they were the ones who derived the greatest measure of benefits from their support. The machine fostered the ethic of power in lower-income whites: politics is a game in which you reward your friends and punish your enemies. Take care of your own.

The primary value-nurturing institution of middle- and upper-class whites has been the reform movement and its parent, the business corporation. The business corporation inculcated the value of efficiency in its participants, and they transferred that value to the political arena, where it served as a guiding principle for the reformers. Government ought to be run like a business, which is to say, without regard for politics or constituent preferences. This entails replacing the "rascals" with experts, whose "value-free" calculations will eliminate the inefficiency and dishonesty which make such a travesty of government under machine rule.

The church has been the primary value-nurturing institution of blacks. Its moral teachings concerning fairness and brotherhood provide a radically different basis for political action. The new black politics uses need, rather than the machine's principle of reciprocity or the reformers' cost-benefit calculations, to establish a system of benefit distribution that is designed to achieve equity. Given the white and middle-class bias of the prevailing distribution system, the new arrangement cuts sharply against the grain, and it entails an acute downward redistribution of benefits. For this reason, the new black politics may best be understood as a lower-class reform style of politics.

When we characterize the new politics in this manner, it should become evident that Mayor Washington faces several formidable obstacles in establishing a reform government based on the ethic of fairness. To begin with, it is an alien and also a threatening proposition to many of the city's white citizens. The presumption of lower-class whites, who have been imbued with the ethic of power, is that Mayor Washington will use the power of his office to empower blacks at the expense of whites. Considering the city's political history, this hardly constitutes an unreasonable expectation. Moreover, since the ethic of fairness entails a substantial downward redistribution of benefits toward the many blacks who occupy the lower rungs of the socioeconomic ladder, the changes will reinforce white perception that Mayor Washington is favoring blacks at the expense of whites. Accordingly, the new mayor will have to make it vividly clear in redressing the imbalance that he is including Latinos and deprived whites in the new distribution scheme. To minimize the sense of loss that those who have benefited from the status quo will feel, the new mayor will also have to implement the changes in an incremental rather than root-and-branch manner.

At the same time, Mayor Washington must take into consideration the needs and expectations of his principal supporters. Lower-income blacks in particular are likely to prefer a redistribution program that is implemented rapidly and that is heavily skewed in their favor. The simple fact is that it is far easier to opt for the ethic of fairness on a full stomach. While the cultural value of fairness serves to unite the black community, the class factor constitutes a divide. The life led along Chicago's low-income black area on near Southside 43rd Street is far harder to bear than the one enjoyed around the city's middle-class black area along far Southside 93rd Street. So it is unsurprising that the values tend to differ.

Voting returns bear out the existence of a sharp black class divide. South of 63rd Street, in the higher-income black wards, the support for reform has been strong. Virtually every one of these wards has at some point put a reform-minded alderman into office. These are also the wards that gave Mayor Washington the most support. It is a different story north of 63rd Street and on the impoverished West Side. Reform has picked up little help in these areas. The principal exception is the strong support they gave Harold Washington. If the new mayor is to turn the exception into the rule, he must demonstrate that the ethic of fairness is preferable in the long run to the more obvious short-term enticements of the ethic of power.

Besides the racial conflict and class problems, Mayor Washington faces an integration problem involving the black middle class. The ethic of fairness supported by the black middle class developed to some extent because of their exclusion from the white corporate opportunity structure. As these barriers are increasingly set aside and knocked down, the blacks who enter the corporate world will acquire greater exposure to the ethic of efficiency and economy. As a result, they may begin to vote their pocketbooks instead of their hearts.

Thus the ethic of fairness sits squarely between the ethic of power and the ethic of efficiency, and blacks are being pulled away from the center in both directions. Mayor Harold Washington's task is to fortify the middle ground. It is a challenge as formidable as any faced by a Chicago mayor. It is equally significant. Equality and fair play are the ideals toward which our system of government is supposed to be directed. So, to the extent that Harold Washington is successful, he will have made a profound contribution to the improvement of life and politics in Chicago.

If we turn now to a more detailed examination of reform in Chicago, it can be seen that the struggle to reform the city's politics has been a lengthy enterprise and that the idea of reform has undergone a significant amount of change. As the social structure of Chicago changed, so too did the backers of political reform and their goals. What had traditionally been the political province of an array of economy-minded, middle-class white citizens from all along the periphery of the city was transformed into, first, a lakefront liberal enterprise, and then a black political movement.

The Changing Shape of Reform in Chicago Politics

The conventional wisdom about political reform is predicated on a pattern of conflict that no longer exists in the big cities. Big-city political conflict traditionally amounted to social class warfare. The middle and upper classes pitted their reform style of politics against the poor who backed the political machine. The conflict centered on the twin issues of efficiency and honesty. The reformers opposed the machine's plundering, its manning of government agencies with party agents, and the provision of public services on an exchange basis: benefits for votes. The reformers wanted to run things on the square, replace the party's agents with professionally trained career civil servants, and dispense services on the basis of cost-efficiency rather than favoritism.[6]

But the conflict involved more than class antagonism. Seething beneath the surface—and frequently bubbling to the top—were the closely related issues of ethnicity and religion. The reformers were not merely affluent; they were overwhelmingly Protestant and Jewish, with roots in England and northern Europe. The low-income backers of the machine, on the other hand, were predominantly Catholics who had immigrated from eastern and southern Europe. The cultural differences served to reinforce the class hostility.

The political sociologist Seymour Martin Lipset has spoken to the significance of the cultural differences. Protestantism, he says, "contributed to individualism, self-reliance, feelings of personal responsibility for success and failure, and interpretation of social evils in terms of moral turpitude." Catholicism, on the other hand, "has tended to stress community responsibility and does not emphasize individual morality."[7] From the cultural perspective of the reformers, then, the problem with the poor was not so much their lack of income as their lack of character. This lack left the poor without the wherewithal to save themselves from the machine's rapacious clutches, and so the burden fell upon the reformers to serve as the poor's liberators. It is not hard to see, however, how the reformers' moral perspective prevented them from securing many allies among the poor.

This classic pattern of conflict no longer dominates big-city politics. The Protestants and their northern European Jewish brethren gave up their responsibilities and fled across the city borders to the suburbs and beyond, leaving the poor to fend for themselves. That exodus eviscerated the reform enterprise. At the same time, the political machine collapsed, largely the victim of reforms inflicted by the Protestants and Jews before they fled the big-city battlefield.

The exodus and the collapse radically altered big-city politics. The instructors, machine and reform, of the old city's residents are no longer around to shape and constrain the political values and behavior of the new city's citizens. This has left blacks and Latinos in particular, who have had the least positive knowledge of and experience with machine and reform politics, largely free to construct their own versions of political reality. Of course, cities are not islands, and so the higher levels of government, as well as big business corporations, have imposed some sharp limitations on the construction possibilities.

Since the establishment of the Democratic political machine in Chicago at the onset of the Great Depression, three significantly different reform coalitions have contested the machine for control of the city's politics. As an indication of just how dynamic Chicago politics has recently become, two of those three reform coalitions have emerged only during the past fifteen years. The stratification framework developed by Max Weber may be employed to identify the essential characteristics of the three reform coalitions. Accordingly, we shall call the three coalitions the class reformers, the party reformers, and the status reformers.[8]

Table I indicates the basic dimensions along which the three reform coalitions differ. The chart can serve as a guide to the following discussion of each of the three coalitions.

TABLE I
The Basic Dimensions of Political Reform: Chicago, 1931-1983[9]

Coalition	Composition	Party Affiliation	Political Goal
1. The Class Reformers	Upper- and middle-class Protestants and northern European Jews	Republican	Governmental efficiency
2. The Party Reformers	Upper- and middle-class Jews and middle-class blacks	Democratic	Political representation
3. The Status Reformers	Upper- to lower-class blacks	Democratic	Socioeconomic equity

The Class Reformers. There is one obvious difficulty in analyzing reform in Chicago politics: there is not very much reform to analyze. Since the formation of the Democratic machine after the mayoral election of Anton Cermak in 1931, Chicago has been essentially a one-party city. The local Republican party, shut out of office, became a skeleton crew, and a good many of those who remained to sail under the Republican flag flew false colors, earning themselves the title of "Republicrats" as a result. After his 1955 defeat, for example, the reform-minded Republican mayoral candidate Bob Merriam complained to a Republican ward boss that only half of the Republican ward committeemen had backed his campaign, whereupon the ward boss informed Merriam that he was overestimating the amount of help that he had actually received. So in the highly pragmatic and treacherous world of Chicago politics the reformers, for the most part, have had to go it alone.

It is, nevertheless, instructive to examine the occasional outcroppings of reform that have surfaced in Chicago's politics. Much can be learned, for example, about the critical relationship that exists between social structure and political style even in a strong-party city such as Chicago. The class reform coalition comprised the reform opposition to the machine during the forty-year period from 1931 all the way through the 1960s; during that period the class reformers put up two mayoral candidates against the machine. In 1939, Republican lawyer Dwight Green was slated to take on the machine's formidable Mayor Edward Kelly. Though Green lost the battle, his strong showing propelled him into the governor's office one year later. In 1955 the reformers backed a Democrat, Alderman Robert Merriam, as the Republican mayoral candidate, which reflected the almost total demise of the GOP organization. Merriam went up against Richard J. Daley, the Democrat machine's party boss, who was making his first bid to combine the jobs of boss and mayor.

Despite the spread of years between the two elections and the vastly different backgrounds of the two candidates, several common threads tie the two elections together. The wards that provided the nucleus of support for the two reformers were virtually identical. Nine of the ten wards that gave Merriam his greatest support had also been the principal backers of Green's candidacy. Both candidates also received about the same degree of citywide support. Green picked up 44 percent of the vote, while Merriam managed 45 percent. The socioeconomic and cultural patterns of conflict were also the same for both elections. The wards that backed the two reformers were almost invariably affluent and mainly Protestant or northern European Jewish. The wards that backed the machine most heavily were populated by Catholics and eastern European Jews. Table II fills in the socioeconomic particulars of the support received by the two reformers.

The two class reform candidates received strong support from all four quadrants of the city: the Northwest and Southwest sides, as well as the Northeast and Southeast lakefront areas. However, these wards were remarkably homogeneous, being either predominantly Protestant or northern European Jewish. Thus, the two elec-

TABLE II

The Class Reformers' Mayoral Elections –
Reform Support and Socioeconomic Rank: Chicago, 1939 and 1955[10]

1939			1955		
Ward	Plurality	Socioeconomic Rank (quartile)	Ward	Plurality	Socioeconomic Rank (quartile)
50	7,042	1st	41	15,583	1st
47	6,621	1st	50	9,807	1st
41	6,564	1st	7	9,761	1st
19	6,552	1st	19	8,589	1st
8	4,517	1st	47	7,446	1st
38	4,130	2nd	49	7,294	1st
36	4,087	3rd	8	5,328	1st
49	4,012	1st	39	4,946	1st
7	3,944	1st	38	4,473	2nd
39	2,060	1st	5	4,334	1st

Source: The election returns were supplied by the Chicago Board of Election Commissioners. The socioeconomic rankings were compiled from the 1940 and 1960 editions of the *Local Community Fact Book* (Chicago: University of Chicago Press).

tions reflect the traditional machine-reform conflict in its classic form.

The two most affluent communities on the Southwest Side, Beverly and Morgan Park, which comprised the bulk of the 19th Ward, were overwhelmingly Protestant. Three of the four Northwest Side wards—the 38th, 39th, and 41st—were also predominantly Protestant. The exception to the rule on the Northwest Side was the lower-income 36th Ward—the only top reform ward to rank in the third socioeconomic quartile. It had a substantial German and Norwegian Protestant population; but the bulk of the ward consisted of Italian and Polish Catholics.

The three reform wards on the Northeast Side—the 47th, 49th, and 50th—housed an affluent Protestant and Jewish population. The 47th Ward consisted mainly of German and Swedish Protestants. The 49th Ward also contained a predominantly Swedish and German Protestant population, but with a sizable Russian and German Jewish population as well. During the 1940s, however, the Protestants began their exodus from the city, leaving the 49th Ward with an increasingly eastern European Jewish population. A similar development took place in the neighboring 50th Ward.

Two of the three Southeast Side reform wards—the 5th and the 7th—were predominantly Jewish. The 5th Ward contained the Hyde Park community, where the University of Chicago is located. The South Shore community made up a large part of the 7th Ward. The other Southeast Side reform ward—the 8th—housed a mixed Protestant-Catholic population of Swedish and Irish residents for the most part.

Besides their class and cultural homogeneity, these reform wards were united in their support of the Republican party and the economy-minded goals the party stood for. During this period virtually all of the City Council reformers were Republicans—the notable exception being the liberal Democrat from the 5th Ward, Bob Merriam—and the newspapers of the day captured the essential spirit of the Council reformers by labelling them the "economy bloc." They sought a government that operated at peak efficiency and was stripped down to delivering the bare essentials, and often even less than that.

The class reformers displayed only limited and fitful concern for the plight of the poor. Martin Meyerson and Edward Banfield have captured the narrow and largely indifferent perspective of the class reformers in their study of the politics of public housing in Chicago.[11] The class reformers were content to deliver the same shoddy goods to the city's school children. A member of the Board of Education at the time complained that Chicago had only two kinds of schools: second rate and third rate. A Council reformer of liberal Democratic persuasion explained why: he blamed the city's political and economic elite for their single-minded preoccupation with holding down government's costs to the virtual exclusion of any regard for quality.[12] It is little wonder, then, that the class reformers received so little support for their reform goals from the city's poor.

The Party Reformers. Bob Merriam's 1955 mayoral campaign turned out to be the last hurrah for the class reform coalition. Thereafter, with the exception of the Polish maverick Benjamin Adamowski's run in 1963, the Republican party slated only guaranteed losers against Mayor Daley, and the reformers ran no candidates of their own during the 1960s. A handful of reformers continued to win seats in the City Council; but their small numbers prevented them from being anything more than gnats on the hard hide of the machine.

Yet the decline of Republican and reform voting during the 1960s is not simply attributable to the Democratic machine's strength and skill. Much of the machine's success was due to a profound series of demographic changes that radically altered the city's political landscape. The exodus of middle- and upper-class Protestants and northern European Jews that had begun in earnest following World War II continued apace throughout the fifties and sixties. The class reform enterprise perished in the process.

If we examine the communities that housed the city's socioeconomic elite at the outset of the 1950s, we can readily see the effect of the exodus twenty years later. All but three of Chicago's top twenty elite communities experienced a decline in their executive-professional population. Table III provides the particulars of the occupational decline of the city's elite communities.

Table III's figures indicate that only two areas of the city experienced an increase of executives and professionals: Hyde Park and the near Northside communities of Lakeview and Near North.[13] There is a significant political corollary to this development. Hyde Park and the near North Side became the twin islands of reform during the 1970s. William Singer and Dick Simpson, the two leading Northside reformers, both represented near Northside wards; the leading Southside reformer, Leon Despres, represented Hyde Park. Meanwhile, reform had collapsed in the other elite communities.

It is equally instructive to examine cultural change in the city's elite communities. For, as we have said, reform is not merely a class-based enterprise; it is a cultural phenomenon as well. Table IV indicates that the cultural shifts that took place in the elite communities were as instrumental in altering the course of reform as were the occupational changes.

Table IV reveals that three distinct cultural shifts took place during this twenty-year period. The Northeast Side, especially along the lakefront, became increasingly populated by eastern European Jews, primarily Russian Jews. In the two Northwest Side communities closest to the lakefront, North Park and Albany Park, a similar change occurred. The Swedish and, to a lesser extent, the German Protestants departed the Northeast Side for the suburbs. A good many of the Germans who remained were Jewish; thus the principal shift here was from Protestant to Jewish.

A similar departure of Protestants took place on the northwest side of the city. However, here the Protestants were replaced by Catholics, most notably Poles and Italians, who like large numbers of the eastern European Jews had migrated out from the inner city as their income and housing opportunities improved. The inner-city Jews went east to the lakefront, while the Catholics headed to the

TABLE III
Occupational Change in Chicago's Elite Communities, 1950-1970

Community	Professional and Executive Population		Change
	1950	**1970**	
Northeast Side			
Rogers Park	43.4	35.0	− 8.4
West Ridge	47.8	37.4	−10.4
Uptown	30.1	26.1	− 4.0
Lincoln Square	27.5	22.3	− 5.2
Lakeview	25.6	27.2	+ 1.6
Near North	25.6	41.0	+15.4
Northwest Side			
Edison Park	39.7	24.2	−15.5
Norwood Park	26.8	23.7	− 3.1
Forest Glen	48.4	40.8	− 7.6
North Park	45.0	37.6	− 7.4
Albany Park	31.6	19.0	−12.6
West Side			
Austin	26.6	15.0	−11.6
Southeast Side			
Kenwood	31.9	25.9	− 6.0
Hyde Park	47.1	52.3	+ 5.2
South Shore	43.0	20.6	−22.4
Chatham	31.9	14.9	−17.0
Avalon Park	33.2	19.9	−13.3
Southwest Side			
Beverly	52.9	43.0	− 9.9
Washington Heights	28.2	16.3	−11.9
Morgan Park	29.1	23.9	− 5.2

Source: *1950 Local Community Fact Book* (Chicago: University of Chicago Press, 1953) and *Community Area Data Book* (Chicago: Chicago Assoc. of Commerce and Industry and OSLA Financial Services Corp., no date).

far Northwest Side. Large numbers of Irish Catholics, accompanied by many blacks, similarly displaced the city's Protestant population on the far Southwest Side. Affluent Beverly became an Irish stronghold, Washington Heights a black community, while Morgan Park took on an integrated character. But the general Northwest and Southwest corners shift was from Protestant to Catholic.

The most visually dramatic cultural shift took place on the city's Southeast Side. Blacks, traditionally confined to a narrow "black belt," swept across the Southeast Side following the U.S. Supreme

TABLE IV

Cultural Change in Chicago's Elite Communities, 1950-1970[14]

Community	Predominant Ethnic/Racial Groups in the Community	
	1950	**1970**
Northeast Side		
Rogers Park	Russian, German	Russian, Polish
West Ridge	Russian, Swedish, German	Russian, Polish
Uptown	Swedish, Russian, German	Russian, German
Lincoln Square	German, Swedish	Greek, German
Lakeview	German, Swedish	German, Russian
Near North	Italian, German	German, Russian
Northwest Side		
Edison Park	German, Swedish	Polish, German, Italian
Norwood Park	Polish, German, Swedish	Polish, German, Italian
Forest Glen	German, Swedish	German, Polish, Italian
North Park	Russian, Swedish, Polish	Russian, Polish
Albany Park	Russian, Polish	Polish, Russian, German
West Side		
Austin	Italian, Irish	Italian, Greek
Southeast Side		
Kenwood	German, Russian	Black
Hyde Park	German, Russian	German, Russian, Black
South Shore	Russian, Swedish	Black
Chatham	Swedish, Irish, Hungarian	Black
Avalon Park	Swedish, Irish, German	Black
Southwest Side		
Beverly	German, Swedish, Canadian	Irish, Polish
Washington Hts.	Irish, German, Swedish	Black
Morgan Park	Swedish, German, Irish	Black, Irish, German

Source: *1950 Local Community Fact Book* (Chicago: University of Chicago Press, 1953) and *Community Area Data Book* (Chicago: Chicago Assoc. of Commerce and Industry and OSLA Financial Services Corp., no date).

Court's decision in 1948 that racially restrictive housing covenants were unconstitutional. The sweep was further propelled by a huge population increase. The city's black population stood at just under 500,000 in 1950; by 1970 blacks constituted one-third of Chicago's population, numbering in excess of one million.

Along the lakefront, in the communities of Kenwood and South Shore, blacks replaced a predominantly Jewish community. In the inland communities of Chatham and Avalon Park, blacks replaced a mixed Protestant-Catholic population of mainly Swedish and Irish ancestry (many of the departing Irish headed southwest to Beverly and Morgan Park). Hyde Park was the sole exception to the racial transformation. It used the resources of the federal urban renewal program and the influence of the political University of Chicago to retain a substantial segment of its affluent white population.

As might be anticipated, the political fallout from class and cultural changes of this magnitude was heavy. The changes transformed reform from a conservative, Republican-connected enterprise that was backed by a citywide coalition of the middle and upper classes into a much more narrowly based lakefront liberal Democratic affair. Political reform had been turned on its head.

There were two reform elections during the 1970s, and both indicate the wide scope and radical character of the break with the past. In 1971, a Jewish liberal Democrat, Richard Friedman, challenged Mayor Daley. As Robert Merriam had in 1955, Friedman adopted the colors of the Republican party for the occasion. Then, in 1975 another Jewish liberal Democrat, Alderman William Singer of the near Northside 43rd Ward, took on the mayor. Recognizing the extent to which the backers of reform had become heavily Democratic, Singer challenged Daley in the Democratic party's primary election instead of the general election. Table V details the social class backing that the two reformers received and the outcome of the new reform challenges.

The most obvious characteristic of the new party reform was its narrow range of appeal and attendant weakness. Its success was limited to the Hyde Park and near Northside areas of the city; everywhere else in the city the support was no better than moderate. The backing for the new reform stood in sharp contrast to that for the old reform, which had supporters in all four quadrants of the city.

It is interesting to note that fully one-half of the wards that had been the principal backers of class-based reform were no longer among the supporters of the new party reform. Indeed, some of the old reform wards, notably the far Southwest Side 19th Ward, had become a part of the political machine's principal base of support. The new political orientation of the old reform wards—all of which were on the Northwest and Southwest sides of the city—is due in part to the class-cultural shifts that had occurred in these areas. The new residents of the old reform wards were Catholic instead of Protestant and lower on the socioeconomic scale than the old resi-

TABLE V

The Party Reformers' Mayoral Elections – Reform Support and Socioeconomic Rank: Chicago, 1971 and 1975

1971 General Election			1975 Democratic Primary		
Ward	Plurality	Socioeconomic Rank (quartile)	Ward	Plurality	Socioeconomic Rank (quartile)
5	+1,915	1st	43	+4,569	1st
43	+ 976	1st	5	+3,706	1st
48	−2,587	1st	44	+ 31	1st
44	−3,056	1st	49	− 276	1st
46	−3,470	1st	21	− 522	2nd
8	−3,551	2nd	8	− 761	2nd
21	−3,756	2nd	48	− 859	1st
6	−3,814	2nd	50	−1,005	1st
49	−3,837	1st	46	−1,253	1st
7	−4,848	2nd	17	−1,312	3rd

Source: The electoral data supplied by the Chicago Board of Election Commissioners. The socioeconomic rankings were compiled from the *Community Area Data Book* (Chicago: Chicago Assoc. of Commerce and Industry and OSLA Corp., no date).

dents had been. The political fortunes of the machine and reform waxed and waned in the process.

The goals of the new reformers also served to reshape the support structure. The old reform had focused upon increased government efficiency and economizing as its chief objective. The new reform concerned itself largely with the restructuring of the Democratic party in general, and in particular with more equitable representation in the party, notably for blacks and women. Hence the designation of the new reform coalition as the party reformers.

The great symbolic act of the party reformers was the ouster of the city's regular Democratic delegates by the Bill Singer-Jesse Jackson coalition at the 1972 presidential nominating convention in Miami Beach. The ouster dramatically announced to Chicago's white ethnics that they were out and to blacks that they were in—at least as junior partners—in the new party reform coalition. Thus the old reform wards, now populated by white ethnics, had more than one reason for becoming the new machine wards.

In turn, given the party reformers' Democratic orientation and emphasis on equitable representation, they finally offered blacks a reasonable basis for supporting political reform. As Table V indicates, a number of black voters did back the party reform candidates. Richard Friedman ran well in the 6th, 7th, 8th, and 21st wards (all of which were middle-class black wards) and in the 5th Ward, which contained a sizable black middle-class population. Singer also ran well in the black middle-class wards. His black support is all the more impressive because he had to contest the liberal black Democratic state senator, Richard Newhouse, for votes. Singer wound up with far more black votes than did Newhouse. Thus the city's black Protestants had taken the place of the white Protestants in the reform process.

Yet the bottom line on the party reform enterprise is that it never got off the ground. After Singer's abject performance in 1975, the party reformers packed it in. Not even the death of Mayor Richard Daley was able to resuscitate the party reformers for one more effort. The special election in 1977 to select a successor to Daley produced four candidates; none of them was a reformer. Jane Byrne did run successfully as something of a reformer in 1979, but her effort was a media stunt rather than a reform campaign. Hardly any of the city's reform activists participated in what she had of a campaign. When Byrne promptly turned her back on her reform pledges, it seemed clear that Chicago was not ready for reform by hook or by crook.

The Status Reformers. In his 1975 study of the Chicago machine, *Don't Make No Waves, Don't Back No Losers,* Milton Rakove predicted that reform had no future in Chicago's politics.[15] Rakove was well aware of the critical increase in the city's black and Latino population; but he concluded that the "new immigrants" would support the machine just as strongly as the "old immigrants," the white ethnics, once had. For the decisive factor, in Rakove's view, was not color or ethnicity; it was poverty. Thus the machine would prevail because it was able to serve the needs of the poor far more effectively than reform ever had.

Just as Rakove's study was published, two interesting test cases emerged that appeared to support his prediction. Chicago's first black mayoral candidate, State Senator Richard Newhouse, a liberal Democrat from the Hyde Park area, stepped forward to challenge Mayor Daley in 1975 in the Democratic primary. Newhouse's performance was in keeping with Rakove's prediction. He ran a distant third behind Daley and Bill Singer, failing to capture even a second place in any of the black wards.

Two years later, following Daley's death, State Senator Harold

Washington, a black machine maverick, took on Daley's successor, Michael Bilandic. Washington did much better. In a poorly financed and poorly organized effort, he managed to carry most of the middle-class black wards. However, the poor black wards stayed with the machine, and Washington picked up only a small number of white votes, mainly from the liberal Hyde Park area. It was clear that Chicago was highly polarized along racial lines and that poor blacks found the machine's material benefits more relevant to their needs than were the primordial ties of race.

Yet when one views these twin developments from a different perspective, one sees some serious questions surfacing about Rakove's prediction. The two campaigns did constitute a radical break with the past. Under the leadership of Congressman William L. Dawson, blacks had always worked quietly and patiently for progress within the party. They never demanded much more than the machine's leadership was willing to concede, and they never, never raised the issue of race in public. The Newhouse and Washington campaigns said, in effect, that the old rules no longer applied. Washington's harsh and fiery criticism of the machine's unjust treatment of the black community resurrected the leadership style of the "fighting race man."[16] As Washington began to move toward center stage, he pushed the ghost of Dawson's counsel of patience into the wings. The issue no longer was the size of the black community's slice of the pie, but who should be doing the carving.

The defection of central black leaders such as Ralph Metcalfe and Harold Washington from the machine and the strong criticism they and other black leaders directed at the machine's treatment of the black community were undoubtedly crucial in legitimizing reform as an acceptable alternative to the machine style of politics. Yet there is no denying the decisive role played by Jane Byrne in moving blacks toward reform. She began by teaching black voters that they were more powerful and independent in their political judgment than they had been led to believe. For it had been her remarkably strong support from black voters that had enabled her to narrowly defeat the machine. The victory signaled a new political day for blacks. Never again would a mayor dare treat the black community with the contempt that Michael Bilandic had.[17]

Then, after Byrne had raised black political expectations to an unprecedented level, she introduced her second lesson—a virtual textbook on the production of political estrangement. She turned her back on both the reforms she had promised and the black community. She embraced the machine and the "evil cabal" that she had defeated, and she courted the white ethnic voters who had failed to support her candidacy against the machine. Thus, despite the heavy backing blacks had given Byrne, the game remained the same: blacks still were merely marginal players in a political contest between and for the benefit of whites.

Mayor Byrne turned out to be an exceptional instructor. A well-organized and well-financed series of voter registration drives in the black community, which began during the summer of 1982, produced more than 100,000 new black voters. Several new black protest organizations were spawned by one or another of Mayor Byrne's rash actions, and old-line black organizations were re-energized. Jesse Jackson's Operation P.U.S.H. led a black boycott of ChicagoFest, the brightest star in Mayor Byrne's grand constellation of extravaganzas. Harold Washington, who had moved up to Congress in 1980 and emerged as the black community's political leader without peer, announced that he would seriously consider running for mayor, provided the registration drives underway proved to be a success. All of a sudden, the unthinkable was at hand. The apolitical had become political, and the political were in a frenzy. The black community was in full and open revolt, making that wildest of prospects—a black mayor—a genuine possibility.

Therefore, it was not surprising that when Harold Washington finally declared his candidacy, he announced that he would be entering the race as a reformer. Mayor Byrne, with the able assistance of the vocal black leadership that had emerged, had transformed the machine into the black community's enemy. It quickly became apparent, however, that Washington's conception of reform was fundamentally at odds with the earlier reform goals. Class reform's emphasis on economical government and party reform's focus on "good" government had been geared to the interests of the middle class; neither reform movement had displayed much concern for the problems of the disadvantaged. In effect, they had conceded the votes of the disadvantaged to the machine and had gone hunting where the reform "ducks" are to be found: in the middle-class neighborhoods and the affluent lakefront high-rises.

Washington was unwilling to grant the machine such a concession. Instead, he challenged the machine on its own turf by arguing that his reforms would better serve the interests of the disadvantaged. He defined reform in terms of achieving fairness and equity, notably for the city's poor and those who had experienced the greatest discrimination: blacks, Latinos, and women. Thus, whereas the two earlier reform movements had based their appeal primarily on class and ideology, Washington was seeking to form a status-reform coalition by appealing to those with the lowest status in both the city's and the machine's hierarchy of deference.

Forming the status-reform coalition was a high-risk proposition. The poor in general and low-income blacks in particular, who formed the coalition's core, were the most difficult voters to mobilize; and when the poor did vote, they had gone heavily for the machine. Only one of the five "old 'Boss' Dawson" wards on the near South Side had ever elected a reform alderman, and even that had been largely a fluke.[18] Of the four black "plantation" wards on the West Side, only the 29th Ward had shown an inclination to support reform. Needless to say, not many of the low-income white wards would be crossing over to support a black mayoral candidate. Race had displaced reform and party politics years ago as the city's great political divide.

It was also unclear how the affluent white lakefront liberals would respond to the new reform. Status reform certainly was liberal and Democratic, in keeping with the thrust of party reform; yet it clearly went well beyond what the party reformers had in mind. Party reform was one thing; social and economic reforms were something else. As it turned out, the only member of the north lakefront's party reform leadership who backed Washington during the primary election was Dick Simpson, the former alderman of the near north 44th Ward. Washington, nevertheless, was able to field a strong campaign organization in the lakefront wards. The conflict between status reform and party reform was producing new political fault lines along the lakefront.

Table VI indicates the principal backers of the new status reform. All of the wards were predominantly black; only the 4th and 5th wards contained sizable white populations. Only one of the West Side wards, the 24th Ward, showed up in the principal support group. There also was considerable carry-over from party to status reform. Half of the wards that had most heavily backed party reform also provided the greatest support for status reform. But the chief distinguishing characteristic of the new status reform is the strong support it received from the low-income wards that historically had formed the backbone of the machine's structure of support.

The numbers indicate that status reform has a far stronger base of central support than class reform or party reform had been able to form. Overall, the status reform candidate carried twenty wards in the primary, and in the general election he picked up two more wards: the heavily Mexican 22nd ward and the 31st, with its large

TABLE VI

The Status Reformers' Mayoral Elections – Reform Support and Socioeconomic Rank: Chicago, 1983

Democratic Primary			General Election		
Ward	Plurality	Socioeconomic Rank (quartile)	Ward	Plurality	Socioeconomic Rank (quartile)
6	22,917	2nd	6	34,812	2nd
21	21,998	2nd	21	32,687	2nd
8	20,195	2nd	8	30,648	2nd
34	19,266	2nd	17	29,058	3rd
17	17,536	3rd	34	29,036	2nd
20	14,699	3rd	20	25,493	3rd
3	13,783	4th	16	25,433	4th
9	13,126	3rd	3	24,294	4th
5	12,924	1st	24	24,136	4th
4	12,854	2nd	9	22,555	3rd

Source: The Chicago Board of Election Commissioners supplied the electoral data. The socioeconomic rankings are based on the 1980 Census Reports as compiled by the Department of Planning, City of Chicago.

Puerto Rican population. This total of twenty-two wards compares favorably with the performance of the top class-reform candidate. In 1955, Robert Merriam carried twenty-one wards. It, of course, far outdistanced the performance of the party-reform candidate, Richard Friedman, who narrowly carried only two wards. Thus, both in terms of the intensity and scope of support, status reform constitutes the most formidable reform movement in Chicago's history.

Status reform turned political tradition on its head in the lower-income wards of color. Poor blacks and Latinos alike broke their long-standing relationship with the machine and allied themselves with the status-reform candidate. Yet in other parts of the city the traditional political allegiances remained remarkably intact. We can gain some insight into these continuities by making a final comparison: the support given by the old class-reform and party-reform wards to party and status reform.

The north lakefront liberal wards, which formed the core of the party-reform coalition, were the celebrated battleground of the 1983 election. They constituted the vital swing vote in a closely contested race. They also represented an interesting test case of the extent to which anxieties about race could be reconciled with the appeals of reform. Recognizing the high level of racial anxiety that existed, the Bernard Epton camp made the issue the cornerstone of its campaign in both its television commercials and in the precincts. But when the votes finally came in, nothing much had changed along the lakefront. The status-reform candidate received essentially the same level of support that had been given to the party reformer Richard Friedman in 1971.

The Epton campaign's strategy produced much better results in the old class-reform wards on the Northwest and Southwest sides. Yet here too there was more continuity than discontinuity. The intensity changed, but the direction of support remained the same. For the fact is that by the late 1960s the old class-reform wards had become the new machine wards (see Table VII). In part, the shift was a result of the profound class-cultural changes that had occurred in these areas. The altered character of the machine also was a factor. It no longer made many pretensions about being a party of the "little man." By the late 1960s it had become largely a series of conservation programs for the city's white ethnic communities. So there was little sympathy left for any kind of reform in the old class-reform wards. In 1983 race drove Chicago's electorate and its city's political machine and in the process exposed to all the changing face of reform—Chicago-style.

TABLE VII

Electoral Support for Party and Status Reform by the Party-Reform and Class-Reform Wards

Party-Reform Wards	Friedman's Vote	Washington's Vote	Change
43	52.0	35.9	−16.1
44	42.9	39.3	− 3.6
46	40.3	47.0	+ 6.7
48	43.5	43.5	none
49	42.3	43.1	+ 0.8
Total	44.5	41.3	− 3.2
Class-Reform Wards			
19	31.4	20.1	−11.3
36	28.9	4.9	−24.0
38	30.1	6.1	−24.0
39	33.0	14.1	−18.9
41	38.0	7.3	−30.7
Total	32.3	9.9	−22.4

Source: Chicago Board of Election Commissioners.

1. The conventional wisdom about reform politics is conveniently summarized in a chapter of Edward C. Banfield and James Q. Wilson, *City Politics* (Cambridge: Harvard University Press, 1963).

2. I am unprepared to construct a philosophical or precise definition of the term "fairness." In commonsense terms it is readily distinguishable from the machine's exchange and the reformers' cost-efficiency principles of distribution.

3. See, for example, my "The Daley Legacy: A Declining Politics of Party, Race, and Public Unions," in Samuel K. Gove and Louis H. Masotti, eds., *After Daley: Chicago Politics in Transition* (Urbana: University of Illinois Press, 1982).

4. Archibald Carey was the Republican-backed alderman of the 3rd Ward from 1947 to 1954, when he was defeated in the great Democratic landslide of 1955. See my *Black Politics in Chicago: The Quest for Leadership, 1939-1979* (Chicago: Loyola University of Chicago, 1980).

5. The Daley administration performed a leadership role in fostering and maintaining racial discrimination. Numerous successful lawsuits charging racial discrimination were filed against the city in the areas of public housing, the police and fire departments, and the public schools.

6. Not all of the reformers pursued these goals, as historian Melvin Holli has shown. A Detroit reform mayor during the 1890s instituted a range of social reforms on behalf of the immigrant working class, forsaking the typical reform preoccupation with businesslike efficiency and honesty. See Melvin G. Holli, *Reform in Detroit: Hazen S. Pingree and Urban Politics* (New York: Oxford University Press, 1969).

7. Seymour Martin Lipset, "Religion and Politics in American History," in Robert Lee and Martin E. Marty, eds., *Religion and Social Conflict* (New York: Oxford University Press, 1964). Cited in Thomas M. Guterbock, *Machine Politics in Transition* (Chicago: University of Chicago Press, 1980).

8. Max Weber, "Class, Status, Party," in H. H. Gerth and C. Wright Mills, eds., *From Max Weber, Essays in Sociology* (New York: Oxford University Press, 1958).

9. Under "Composition," only the leading supporters of the reforms are listed. The list is not intended to be inclusive of the full range of support.

10. The "Socioeconomic Rank" is based on the percentage of a community area's male population employed in the census categories of professional and manager, the two highest occupational categories. In recognition of the extent to which community area and ward boundaries diverge and of the heterogeneous makeup of most wards, the wards were not ranked individually in the table, but clustered in four quartiles.

11. Martin Meyerson and Edward C. Banfield, *Politics, Planning, and the Public Interest* (Glencoe, IL: The Free Press, 1955).

12. James Clement made the complaint and Leon Despres, then the alderman of the 5th Ward, provided the explanation.

13. One other community area, Lincoln Park, not included in the table, had an increase of professionals and managers. It is located on the near North Side between the Lakeview and Near North communities.

14. The groups represent the leading nationalities of foreign-born as reported by the census bureau.

15. Milton L. Rakove, *Don't Make No Waves, Don't Back No Losers* (Bloomington: Indiana University Press, 1975).

16. On the "fighting race man" leadership style, see Harold Gosnell, *Negro Politicians* (Chicago: University of Chicago Press, 1935) and James Q. Wilson, *Negro Politics* (New York: The Free Press, 1960).

17. Amid strong protest, Bilandic appointed Bennett Stewart, a weak committeeman and outspoken machine loyalist, to the late Congressman Ralph Metcalfe's seat in 1978. During the snowstorm just before the Democratic primary, Bilandic closed the Dan Ryan train stations in the black community in order to improve the flow of train traffic.

18. Fred Hubbard was elected alderman of the 2nd Ward in 1971, a time when the machine's ward organization was in much disarray following "Boss" Dawson's death in November 1970.

Contributors

MELVIN G. HOLLI is Professor of History and director of the Urban Historical Collection at the University of Illinois at Chicago, as well as the author and editor of several books including (with Peter d'A. Jones) *Ethnic Chicago* (1981, 1984) and the *Biographical Dictionary of American Mayors, 1820–1980* (1982).

PAUL M. GREEN is Professor of and director of the Institute for Public Policy and Administration at Governors State University and author of *Illinois Elections* (1979).

RICHARD DAY is director of Richard Day Associates of Evanston, Illinois, a public opinion polling organization that covered the 1982 and 1983 Chicago and Illinois elections for WLS-TV (ABC).

DORIS A. GRABER is Professor of Political Science at the University of Illinois at Chicago and the author and editor of several books including *Mass Media and American Politics* (1980) and *Mass Media Setting in a Presidential Election* (1981).

WILLIAM GRIMSHAW is Associate Professor of Political Science at Ilinois Institute of Technology and author of *Black Politics in Chicago: The Quest for Leadership, 1939–1979* (1980) and *Union Rule in the Schools: Big City Politics in Transformation* (1979).

ROBERT MCCLORY is an Evanston, Illinois, freelance writer who has published a number of pieces of political biography.

MICHAEL PRESTON is Associate Professor of Political Science at the University of Illinois, Urbana, and the author of several studies including *The New Black Politics* (1982).

The late MILTON RAKOVE (deceased, November 1983) was Professor of Political Science at the University of Illinois at Chicago and author of *Don't Make No Waves, Don't Back No Losers* (1975) and *We Don't Want Nobody Nobody Sent* (1979).

DON ROSE is a political consultant, journalist, and keen-eyed observer of the foibles and frailties of political campaigners in cities.

Index